My First Year in the Lord's Family

Liz Kraus

American Literary Press
Five Star Special Edition
Baltimore, Maryland

MY FIRST YEAR IN THE LORD'S FAMILY

Library of Congress
Cataloging-in-Publication Data
ISBN 1-56167-902-X

Library of Congress Card Catalog Number:
2005909741

Published by

American Literary Press
Five Star Special Edition
8019 Belair Road, Suite 10
Baltimore, Maryland 21236

Manufactured in the United States of America

DEDICATION

To my Heavenly Father! Thank you for coming to get me! Thank you for caring about me of all people. A nobody who rejected you! Thank you for being faithful to me even when I turned my back on you! You are so awesome!

To Karl, my very best friend. Thank you for so many things, not the least of which is putting up with me for 11 years and marrying me anyway. Thank you for being my spiritual partner and sounding board. Thank you for trusting the Lord where this book was concerned.

To all of my girls, my precious jewels, so very individual and unique. Thank you for your patience and encouragement while I grow and learn. I am praying for all of you and thanking God for the gift of you everyday.

To my brother and sister and their families, thank you for praying for me. Okay, so it took me a little longer than you in these areas, but I appreciate you not giving up on me.

To my parents, quite simply thank you!

THANK YOU

Newsong for being a big part of my journey back to God. Pick any one of your songs and I have a reason why it mattered to me.

Tom and Wendy O'Connor for being obedient and starting a church and a Bible study in Middletown, Delaware.

Glen and Roe Stuart for sitting with us at the Faith Cafe. You have gained friends for eternity in Karl and I.

Joyce Meyer for holding my hand spiritually while I grew.

Joel Osteen for being my "Happy Minister." My once-a-week dose of pure Joy.

Jesse Duplantis for making me laugh in spite of myself and giving me the courage to be bold when I was unsure.

T D Jakes for waking me up and making me pay attention.

Creflo Dollar for reminding me to "seek the kingdom first."

MY FIRST YEAR IN THE LORD'S FAMILY

*H*ow many testimonies start out, "When I was a child . . ."? Your childhood is your first point of reference for life. No matter what the conditions of your childhood, that is where you started, and you are where you are today because you took steps to get there. Literal and figurative steps.

Listen to children talk sometime and you will see that most often they are concerned with getting somewhere. Unfortunately, for them the somewhere involves getting older:

When I am older - I can walk
When I am older - I can run
When I am older - No more diapers, Yeah!
When I am older - I can ride a bike
When I am older - I can go to school
When I am older - I can be in the play
When I am older - I can drive
When I am older - I can go on my first date
When I am older - I can go to college
When I am older - I can start my career, get married, and have kids (and I can tell them, "When you get older . . .")

Children spend most of their time dreaming about the future. They look forward to it with great anticipation. They can't wait. No fear, no worries, just wonderful things that they **WILL** be able to do when they get there. Faith. Plain and simple. Child-like.

When you listen to adults talk you hear a reverse pattern. The adult is usually looking back at the lack of responsibility and ease of former days. The older the adult is, the further back down the ladder they want to look.

I remember how easy it was - before I had children
I remember how easy it was - before I got married
I remember how easy it was - before I started my career
I remember how easy it was - before I went to college
I remember how easy it was - before I went on my first date
I remember how easy it was - before I learned to drive
I remember how easy it was - before I performed in the school play
I remember how easy it was - before I ever went to school

You can notice a pattern of responsibility shift happening. Children who have very little in their lives in the way of experiences and mistakes are charging forward. The adult who has a life full of experiences and mistakes remembers the times when life seemed easier. Unfortunately, adults are looking back over a road filled with potholes to an easier time.

Some look back and wonder, "what was the purpose?" I hope you are not one of these people, but if you are we have a lot in common. And, if you are, STOP! Take a deep breath! And, have faith! The road crew is on the way to make repairs to the road!

GOD CALLS, YOU ANSWER ... NOW WHAT?

*H*ow about you stop going to church for 20 years? You get married to someone who doesn't know the Lord. You raise two children who don't know the Lord. You destroy that marriage. You meet someone new who doesn't know the Lord. You help raise two additional children who don't know the Lord. You live the high life. You destroy a multimillion dollar business. You go into debt to the tune of $3,000,000.00 (count the zeros!). You lose your country club membership. You lose your assets. You lose people you thought were your friends. You gain immeasurable depression. You gain paralyzing fear. You gain 100 pounds because you spend most of your time sitting on the couch worrying about what happened to your life.

This is what happened to me when I got "saved" in 1984. That's right, I said all that happened *after* I got "saved." What went wrong? Well, that's a long story!

I was raised Catholic. By that, I mean I was told that I was Catholic. I was a relatively normal kid. I had two parents who lived together. I had a younger brother and sister. I didn't like going to church. It took away too much play time. I went to a Catholic school. Not because we could afford it, but because my dad worked at the school. I spent most of my childhood studying religion. I knew the stories of the Bible. I knew about Jesus and what happened to him. I knew God was real, but I believed that God helped those that helped themselves. And that is where "normal" ends.

By the time I was 13, I had spent my entire life in fear! I prayed to a God that didn't answer prayers. I wasn't old enough to help myself so He didn't listen to me. He took away the one thing I could rely on one month before my 13th birthday. My grandmom. Her and my grandpop had been living with us since I was about 9 or 10. God had put me in the most evil household and proved over and over again that there was nowhere to run. There was nowhere to hide.

My dad's frustrations existed on many levels. They were always much larger when he drank. They were usually centered on his responsibilities as a family man. It was very apparent that he had no interest in being a husband or father.

I don't remember a time when my parents didn't drink and fight. I don't remember a time in my childhood when I could depend on having food, electric, water, etc. I don't remember a time when I wasn't afraid to come home. I loved school because it got me out of my house. I don't remember a time when I could invite friends over without worrying the whole time that the bottom was going to drop out and the "secret" would be revealed. I guess because of the nature of the "secret" it didn't drop, but I only tested it rarely.

The big "secret" was that my father was physically, verbally, and emotionally abusive. He would be the big man in public. The great husband. The great father. The great employee. The great Catholic. Everyone liked him. Everyone, that is, except his family. My dad was all about "don't tell anyone anything." There were no domestic violence laws at the time. When the police came to the house, they would ask him if everything was okay and then leave. I couldn't believe it. It should have been obvious to anyone that things were not okay, but their hands were tied.

And about the time I was 12, he started watching Christian television. I'll bet you think the story takes a turn here. It does, but not for the better. Now, not only is he Catholic, but he is Christian. He now has the Bible to back him up. He can prove that he is allowed to do anything he is doing because he has proof from God. He picked out all the scriptures that related to a wife and children and used them as his weapons for the next six years. Luckily for my mom, she was able to get away from him two years later.

That just left me and my brother and sister. Now, before you condemn my mom, let me tell you that I begged her to go for years. I couldn't take it anymore. I was resolved to kill him if he laid a hand on me, but she wouldn't stand up for herself. I wanted her to go before he killed her. She finally did when I was 14.

By this time, my grandmom and grandpop had died. We had lost the house and had to go live with an aunt and uncle. And then had moved to a house in a nearby town.

Now, my uncle was very involved in the Catholic church. He was also very much a family man; they had six children (all older than me). He was a man that ruled with an iron fist. He didn't drink. He had a career, not a job. His wife stayed home and raised their children. He was the kind of man that didn't tolerate much out of anyone. Including my dad.

He insisted on my dad attending Alcoholics Anonymous or we wouldn't be getting any help from their family. My dad was not interested. They also crossed swords over the Catholic vs. Christian issue. Needless to say, we only lasted a few months in their home. Then we moved to a nearby town and settled into living. We had stopped attending Catholic church and were now attending Christian services. Of course, the changes in our lives end with a new home and new church.

Not long after this is when my mom left. She basically became homeless and walked her way back to Delaware, where she had family. I didn't believe it was possible for my father to get worse, but I was soon proven wrong. He wouldn't let us talk to my mom if she called. He wouldn't let us know how to get in touch with her. He was very controlling that way. He acted like this alone would bring her back. It never did, and I was 17 years old before I ever got to talk to her again.

Well, it didn't take long for the job to become a disappointment and we were out on the street again. We had to call another aunt to take us in, and she agreed, but under the same conditions as the other aunt and uncle. Dad would agree to anything at this point, and now the conversations revolved around, "She left me with three kids to take care of . . .", "After all I've been through . . .", "I can't take anymore . . ."

I am now 15 and living again with another family. I have nothing really to call my own, but I am thrilled that the fighting is over. I don't have to worry about coming home to a battered and bruised mom. There is hope for me to escape in the future because my mom escaped.

By the time I was 17, I was only doing things for my dad at gunpoint. Figuratively speaking. I didn't care about him in any way. I truly hated him. Deep down, hated him. I didn't care that, by now, he had actually quit drinking. I didn't care that he had moved us back to Delaware and found a good Christian church. I didn't care that he only wanted me to get saved because he was in fear that I never would. I didn't care if he lived or died! Well, that's not exactly true because I had been praying for him to die a terrible death for years. Just my luck, I had a God that didn't answer my prayers.

So, I went to the church with him and got "saved." Big deal. From what I know about God, I definitely wasn't interested in this. Not only that, but at least at a Catholic church I knew what to do. I knew when to stand and when to kneel and what to respond at the right time. I did not like this church. I especially wanted no part of it if my dad wanted to go there.

I found so many ways of getting out of going to church. I was 18 years old now and so close to my escape that I could taste it. I was working three jobs so I was never out of money. I had a full-time job and two part-time jobs at the mall. I would do anything to stay out of that house. I would come home late and leave early. The way I looked at it, I had done my best to protect my brother and sister for most of my childhood. My brother was now 15 and he could take a turn. I was going to go out and do for myself what no one else would.

I was going to be completely independent. I was not ever

going to depend on anyone for anything. It was my way or the highway. I was in control. When you have no control over your life, it seems to be the most important thing in the world. I worked hard, very hard. I worked my way up at every job I ever had. My bosses could depend on me always. I eventually went to work for a construction company. A very nontraditional industry for a woman. I was going to break every rule and make it work. I got married in 1987 after finding out that I was pregnant. I had already decided that I was not giving up the baby. I was in love with the father, but I didn't care if the father was involved or not; he could marry me or not, but he was going to be a father anyway.

He married me and while I enjoyed playing house in the beginning, it was pretty obvious that he didn't really enjoy the family life. We had good moments, but overall he was not what I expected in a husband. Believe it or not, I had the 1950's image of marriage even though I didn't have the willingness to give up control. We did not have a 1950's marriage. Shortly after my second daughter was born in 1991, I gave up. Plain and simple. I didn't care about this marriage in any way. I swore that my girls were not going to be raised in the same way that I was and I could see us heading that way more and more.

He would have never raised a hand to me, but the signs were there that he was not happy. I was working my way up in my career. He always hated his job. He wouldn't quit, but he hated it just the same. I would never stay at a job I hated. I couldn't understand why he did. I liked my job and would do anything to move up. I would take on anything new they gave me so that I could learn it all. I switched companies so that I could have a better position twice while we were married. I had no tolerance for someone who was willing to just sit around and complain about things as they were and not make the necessary changes. I had already spent my entire life with someone that wasn't happy. I would not spend the rest of my life with some-

Liz Kraus

one like that. He didn't really know this and it's not his fault, it was just my twisted way of thinking.

In 1992 I met someone else who was in the same type of marriage. I worked for him. Now that I look back, I can see how we basically talked each other into ending our marriages. "You shouldn't have to put up with that . . .", "There has to be someone else out there to make me happy . . .", "I can't believe he/she did that . . .", "Why don't you just leave him/her . . ." During this time we were becoming the very best of friends. We sympathized with each other's situations. We had so much in common and we wanted the same things out of life.

In 1993 I finally told my husband to leave. He left; he knew it was over. I turned to my best friend, Karl. He had left his wife about six months earlier and we immediately got together. I realized that the last year of my marriage had been an interview process for the right person. I had never quit a job before securing a position in another company. When I gave notice, it was to prepare for the new job. This wasn't any different.

Karl owned his own construction company. He was relatively successful and he loved his job. He knew what he was doing and was good at it. I was in love, again. The difference was he was interested in all the same things I was. He had really wanted a traditional marriage and a happy home. Up to that point neither of us had found one. We agreed on almost everything. We still do.

Religion came up at some point during our getting-to-know-each-other stage. I was surprised to find out that when he was young he had actually wanted to be a minister. He was raised Methodist and was actually pretty involved with his church until he left his wife. This surprised me because we loved to go to parties. I never really went out much until I met Karl. I did, however, pick it right up. We may have loved the parties a little too much occasionally, but for the most part we just loved being around a lot of happy people all the time. Karl for the most part was the life of any party, so we got invited often.

My First Year in the Lord's Family

By 1996, Karl won emergency custody of his two girls. We joined a predominantly Jewish country club and I learned how to play golf. We were friends or friendly with everyone. Even if we didn't know them, everyone seemed to know us. Our kids were known, too. They all joined the swim team. We were at the club very often. That same year we moved into a very exclusive area. Half of our friends didn't even live this way. We had a home that was 6,000 square feet (or 1,000 square feet per person). We had built the house with the intent of selling it and building something more reasonable for ourselves. The problem was we had built the perfect house for us and our lease was up. What were we going to do?

Well, movin' on up seemed like a good idea. We had a yearly party that everyone loved to attend. It started small in the old house and by the time we moved we were up to more than 100 people that expected invitations. No problem because now we had plenty of room.

Our life was cruising right along. Karl seemed to have the "Midas touch" when it came to work. In my wildest dreams I could never have imagined this life for me. When we weren't working together we were playing together. Our motto seemed to be: Give everything 100%. What is the worst that can happen?

In 1998 we found out. Karl's business started to slide. At first it only seemed like a little glitch in the road, and we always believed that "things would turn around." Unfortunately, they never turned around enough and the business went into a dead fall. By 1999, we could see the writing on the wall. We didn't know what to do so we did little. We didn't let anyone know what was going on; we suffered together silently.

Later that year, the business was closed. The house was taken by the bank and all the assets of the business were sold at auction. And there was still a $3,000,000.00 debt hanging out there. What were we going to do? The business and all the assets had been in Karl's name. The most logical thing to do was start a business in my name. If Karl could do it once, he could do it again.

Over the years, we had discussed getting married. We put it off for various reasons. We even got formally engaged at one of our parties in 1996 on my 30th birthday. We were afraid, plain and simple. Living together was one thing, but getting married was something altogether different. Living together required no commitment. We could leave if we wanted to with no entanglements. Getting married meant stuck. Getting married meant separating would be ugly. Getting married required work. Living together was easy. Living together was fun. Living together meant that no matter what we did we weren't breaking any rules of marriage.

Now we have a failed business and our new excuse was that we didn't want the mistakes we made to affect my credit and our possible future. We started the new business in 1999. Here I was, a president of a construction company. I worked my way up from being a receptionist to owning my own construction business. Men were going to work for me now. Now they were going to do it my way. And my way was, of course, the right way. I was finally in control.

Something had been plaguing me for so long and I didn't even know what it was. I was recovering from all of this life and I now know I knew something was wrong. I couldn't quite put my finger on it, but something was really missing. I always felt depressed and worried. I always felt empty. My daughters would tease me about crying over every happy ending in a movie. It was so bad that I could cry at a touching commercial.

This was a real problem for me. The reason they made such a big deal out of my crying is because no one ever saw me cry. I never cried in front of anyone if I could help it. I used every excuse known to man for tearing. Sinuses, yawning, smoke in my eyes (I am a smoker). You name it and I had an excuse. They competed to see who could buy me a card that would make me cry. I avoided crying by only pretending to read the cards. I only ever actually read the cards in private later. While I'm writing this, no one to this day knows that secret.

I was tough; I was resilient; I was smart; and I was going to raise daughters that were the same. No man would ever be able to out maneuver any of my girls. They were going to be the most independent women on the market. They were going to be wanted for their strength and courage. They were going to be known for their no-nonsense attitude. I would bring them up smart no matter what it cost.

I was truly wounded in the pride department while driving my daughters to school one morning in 2001. We listened to all the cool teenage radio stations. I knew all the words to every boy band and teeny-bop pop singers' music. I was a cool mom. I liked their music and we talked about everything. My daughters kept very little close to the vest, mostly because they knew I would help them handle different situations.

I became the mom to watch when a certain song came on the radio. It was Christmastime in 2001, and a song came on that made me fall apart almost to the point of having to pull the car over. The song was "Christmas Shoes," by Newsong. I am prepared to do a lot of name dropping in this story because I believe they all need to know that they matter. They should keep fighting the good fight.

Well, I listened to this song and I couldn't see to drive. I immediately had a feeling that I should do something for someone less fortunate. Of course, I didn't. What I did do, however, was buy that CD for everyone I felt comfortable giving it to. I had a close friend who recently lost her husband and I gave it to her suggesting she listen to "God & Time." I gave it to another couple who were good friends of ours and asked them to listen to "Sheltering Tree." I bought a copy of the CD for both my brother and sister. And I bought it for a friend of my oldest daughter.

This was the beginning of the end for me. I see that now, but at the time I just thought it was a pretty cool CD and it happened to be a Christian CD. It was a turning point, but I didn't see what was going on. I felt the grasping in my soul but wouldn't give in to it for anything. I just kept on living my life the way I had been.

In 2003, I realized that the new company we had started was falling apart. We had laid off both of our salaried people. These were the two out of three employees that were in charge of the jobs. Once they were both gone, Karl would be solely responsible for managing the jobs. There was no way that he could be in more than one place at a time. Worse than that, we had no work for more than six months. We couldn't get any of our former customers to talk to us. We couldn't seem to find work anywhere. There was construction work going on all over Delaware and we didn't have one project.

We borrowed to keep the electric on in our house. We borrowed to make all of the bills. We were back in our slide and I was going to lose my mind. I had already been holding on to shreds of my sanity from losing the last business. I knew that the debt was still hanging out there—it was not going to go away. We are now going to add insult to serious injury. I fell apart. I was totally lost. I realize that other people saw how we lived and wished they had the problems we had, but they didn't understand. They didn't know the truth; they knew what we let them see. For the second time in my life, I saw the writing on the wall.

Have you ever been up against a situation that you couldn't avoid and desperately wanted to? Were you ever at the end of your nerves to the point where you were paralyzed with fear waiting for the inevitable? Have you ever been in a situation where you didn't know what to do so you did nothing? Have you ever been so embarrassed that you could barely face your family or closest friends? Have you ever been in a situation where you didn't know where to turn because you were beyond help? Have you ever played the lottery hoping for your miracle? Have you ever gotten to the point where you were willing to sell everything you had to get even, and no one would buy? Have you ever been totally hopeless and you really knew this deep down inside of you?

If you have, then have I got news for you!

CAN I HAVE A SECOND CHANCE?

I actively asked God for help in the middle of 2003. I will never forget sitting up late one night on my couch praying and desperately crying. "God, this can't be happening! You can't possibly want this for me! Even if Karl is not the right person for me (I had been told this by everyone), I know You don't want to lose him. What am I supposed to do? Haven't I done enough yet? Haven't I worked hard enough? I know I am a horrible person, I've been told, but is there no chance for me? Are You trying to ruin me completely? Am I destined to be homeless? Is our family just cursed for generations and we have to live with it? Is there nothing I can do to please You?"

I believe this was the first time I desperately cried out to God in twenty years! And my book actually begins here.

My first year in the Lord began in the end of 2003. Like I said before, I was at the end of my rope and had nowhere to turn. I spent several nights crying out to God to help me get back to Him. I knew I needed to find a church. I don't know how I knew, I just knew. Karl had been raised Methodist, so I knew picking the church was the first obstacle. It had to be Bible-based, but if the services were intimidating Karl would never come back. The church I had attended in the past was so large and the praise and worship seemed so out of control that I had felt overwhelmed. I knew Karl would not stay for one entire service, let alone get saved.

When I prayed to God about a church I specifically asked for a church in my area where Karl would be comfortable. I needed a church that I could be accepted in and, to me, it was just as important that Karl be accepted. Just in case he might be interested. Of course, his interest didn't really matter to me because I needed it. I needed something, and I was determined to give this a try. Karl's needs were really secondary.

I had learned some things from the Christian churches that I had attended in the past. I had learned that God always listens. He doesn't always answer, "yes," but He always listens. I figured He would listen to me on this because I was looking for Him. I was not sure how to find my answer, but I was going to ask anyway.

Surprisingly, in December I was reading a newspaper that I hardly ever read and I saw an advertisement in the church listing. A new nondenominational, Bible-based church was coming to our area in January. The first service would be on January 4th at 6:30 p.m. in the senior center. I looked up! I looked all the way up and said, "Well, that is one way to answer a prayer!"

I re-read the ad and realized what God had done. This was a brand new church. Not only would I attend for the first time, but everybody would. And I didn't even have to get up early in the morning. What is anyone doing on a Sunday night? Nothing. It is a perfect time! I went to the calendar and wrote down the time and place. I made a promise that I was going with or without Karl.

Going to church hadn't been an issue for the last ten years that we had been together. The Philadelphia Eagles were in the playoffs for the first time since anyone could remember. Karl couldn't see any reason why he really needed to be there. It was going to be without. No problem.

I didn't mind because I was going for me. Whether Karl went wasn't the issue. I needed it. I still wasn't sure if Karl was going to be comfortable there anyway. So I resolved to go and find out. I went and enjoyed the service. I don't really remember what the sermon was about, but one thing happened and I knew I would be back.

The pastor and his wife had recently moved to Delaware

from Philadelphia. The pastor said, "I'm not sure why we are here, but we will stay as long as the Lord directs us." I almost started crying right then. The service was nice. It was subdued enough that Karl wouldn't feel intimidated. As for me, all I really needed was for it to be Bible-based and it was. I left when the service was over but not before letting the pastor know that the reason they were there was because I had prayed for them to come.

When I got in my car, I thanked God and tried to remember everything about the service. I had to go home and tell Karl. I did, and he seemed ever so slightly interested. I went every Sunday in January and proceeded to come home and tell him what the service was about. He knew that I was happy about going to church. Although he may have had reservations, after the Superbowl he decided to go with me. In February he went, and at the end of the service he told me he would be going back with me. He liked the service and he liked the pastor. We had found a church! God had sent me a church, in my area, where Karl was comfortable. He had answered a prayer!

In March, I decided to sign up for the women's Bible study. We were going to be studying the book *A Woman After God's Own Heart,* by Elizabeth George. I didn't know it at the time but this was going to cause a turning point in my life. I had been **thinking** I was a Christian. The fact that I had no evidence of being a Christian in my life caused me to wonder. I didn't know how to find out, so I went to Bible study every week.

I did my homework. Every chapter in the book had several scripture references. I decided to look them up in my Bible and start writing them out as my notes. I thought that I should have some kind of reference materials when I went to Bible study. I had given the impression that I was a Christian and I didn't want to look like a complete idiot. So, I studied. I read and re-read the chapter. I wrote out the scriptures in longhand and then I typed them up on my computer and started a notebook.

I have always found that I remember things easier when I

write them down. This time was no different. I had the notes in front of me like a cheat sheet but found that I could remember the things I had read without cheating. I was even able to participate in the Bible study without feeling like a fool. This was not the Liz I knew. I was actually excited on Saturday mornings because I was going to Bible study. Saturday mornings were usually spent recovering from Friday nights prior to this time.

I guess it's about time that I start *acting* like a Christian. Where do I start? Little did I know that finding a Bible-based church and joining a Bible study group had been an excellent place to begin. I had Bible study on Saturday. I had church on Sunday. I had also started a prayer journal that I wrote prayers in every day.

Yes, Jesus is my Savior. Yes, I know he has paid the price for my sins. Yes, I know God has forgiven me. Excellent! On an intellectual level, I get it! Now what?

That answer came later that month. Our church decided to hold a social function called a "Faith Café." This is where we all get together on a Saturday night and invite the public in for food and Christian entertainment. Our church is very small. There are only five of us that attend regularly, and of the five, three of us our women. We decided it was our job to plan this function.

We had a meeting to assign various tasks. I told everyone that Karl was an excellent cook. Karl was volunteered to cook his famous baked ziti and meatballs. I volunteered to make the centerpieces. By the end of the meeting all of the tasks were assigned. Everyone knew what they had to do, and the work Karl and I had to do would be finished before the entertainment started. All we had to do was sit back and enjoy the food and the show.

The first act that night was a couple named Glen and Roe Stuart. They go by the name "EXTREME FAITH." They sing and minister using their personal stories and the Gospel. Karl and I both thought they were excellent. Karl was also surprised that they so freely told their story. When they were finished, they sat at our table. These are two people who are on fire for Jesus.

Once we got their ears, we couldn't seem to get enough of them. They were the most loving, honest and straightforward people we had probably ever met. We told them most of our story and they didn't condemn us, they didn't judge. They were simply adamant that we not give up on Jesus. They couldn't seem to get that across enough.

Later in the evening, Karl got a few minutes alone with Glen. Glen asked Karl a life changing question, "Are you saved?" Karl admitted that he didn't know. He told Glen about his religious experiences up to that point. He told Glen that he believed in Jesus and the stories of the Bible. But he wasn't sure he felt saved. God, please bless Glen! Glen said, "Well, you should pray and ask God if you are saved." Plain and simple.

Karl told me about this conversation after we left. I couldn't believe it because I had been praying for Karl in my prayer journal about getting saved. I had been waiting for him to say something, and here we were talking about just that. He said he had been praying every morning in his truck on his way to work. He said the conversations lasted anywhere from five to thirty-five minutes. I didn't know about him praying, so I was thrilled to find out.

The following week I kept my same schedule. Every morning I got up and went to my prayer journal. I prayed for everyone I knew and everyone on our prayer list. On March 25th, I was doing just that when Karl called me. I thought he forgot something because he had left for work only twenty minutes prior to this call. I answered the phone and he sounded out of breath. He told me that he had been taking Glen's advice all week. This morning, however, he got in his truck, and almost as soon as he asked "Lord, am I saved?" this peace came over him so strong. He was laughing and crying at the same time. All this happened before he got to the entrance of our development. He said he knew! He knew for sure that he was saved!

I could barely contain myself. Now I didn't have to do this alone. I had a partner to work with. I was so happy that I wasn't the only one in the house actively searching for God. I could talk to Karl about anything before, and now we had this also. We could share anything we learned and I knew that two heads were better than one. We may be able to catch up to all the other Christians quickly. It's funny to write this now and realize that I actually thought this way.

I had been talking about being a Christian for only three months, but it seemed like a long time. Karl used to say, "You are so far ahead of me." I, of course, was a fraud. I immediately started praying, "What am I going to do?" Karl is asking questions that I can't answer. A real Christian should be able to answer these questions. He didn't realize that in his heart he was actually further along than I was in the trust department. I wasn't even 100% sure that I was saved.

I had been a Christian in absentia for twenty years. I had no answers. I was ill-prepared. I knew some things, of course, but not much. I would encourage him but doubt it all myself. I didn't even know where to begin to find the answers. I ended up limiting us to what we learned at Bible study or in church.

IRON SHARPENS IRON

A funny thing happened in April. I was sitting in my base-
ment doing my Bible-study homework on a Saturday morning. The television was on but I wasn't really paying attention.
Then God introduced me to Christian television. This woman
came on and started telling me how pathetic I was if I said I was
a Christian but acted in various other ways. I stopped doing my
homework. I turned up the television. I fell in love with Joyce
Meyer that morning. I had heard Christian television when I
was little, but I didn't remember them talking like this. Like a
best friend who really cared about you and told you like it was.

She went on to tell me about being religious and being saved.
Apparently there could be a difference. She said there were
people who thought they were saved but really were not. How
am I supposed to know the difference? Tune in next time. I
couldn't believe it! What was I supposed to do now? This woman
can't come on my television and then leave me hanging! Where
does she live?

I did eventually calm down. I figured I would just wait until
next week. I finished my homework and went to Bible study.
For the next two weeks, I searched frantically. I didn't know
the name of the show. I found out later that on my television
listing the name wasn't correctly listed anyway. I was going to
have to call someone.

Everyone in my family knew that I wasn't living a Christian
life. Most of them were saved and eager to preach but I hadn't
ever been really interested. I had been polite and noncommittal.
None of them knew about the last four months of my life. Who
should I call and how was I going to make this phone call?

I called my little sister. We talked all the time. We are the very best of friends. I am still the big sister who knows better and she is the little sister who needs guidance. That works for us. It wasn't, however, going to work for me now. I needed a little help. I figured she could help me, but how do I bring it up?

I called her one afternoon and we talked like always. Sometimes our phone calls lasted five minutes and other times they lasted two hours. This time I was willing to spend some time. I finally got up the nerve and as noncommittally as possible said, "I caught that Joyce Meyer show a couple of Saturdays ago." She was thrilled! She said, "I watch her all the time." My hands were actually sweating. I was so cool and casual when I said, "Oh really? When do you watch her?" She said, "I watch her on such and such a channel at such and such a time." I said, "Oh really? Yeah, she's okay!" In the meantime, I am scrambling around the house. Why can't I find a pencil when I need one? Don't we have any paper in this house?

While I was frantically looking for a way to write this precious morsel of information down, my sister went on to tell me about her show and all the things she had learned from her. She also gave me a list of resources that she had ordered. I was foaming at the mouth while still trying to be cool. I dropped the subject and moved on to other things, and eventually ended the call.

The next morning, after the kids were off to school, I started looking. My sister and I don't have the same cable company so I was going to have to search. I had the name of the show and various stations that carried Christian television. I started my search at 7 a.m. I found her at 9 a.m. I was so excited that I forgot to set the VCR. I had been telling Karl about Joyce Meyer and promised that if I found her show I would tape it for him.

I settled in to watch, and she was working on a series called *Mind, Mouth, Moods and Attitudes*. Of all the series to catch first, this one ministered to me for the next two months. I ordered it by the end of the week. I also ordered *Me and My Big*

Mouth. I couldn't wait to get them.

I thought that Christian television was going to be an answer to a prayer. I would be able to get a little bit of the Word every day. Something to focus on and sink my teeth into. That's not what God had in mind. My sister called, and because the door had been opened, she started asking me questions about my faith. I told her that I didn't really want to make a big deal about it, but that I had been going to church since January. I also told her that Karl was now saved.

She was so excited! Now she had someone she could talk to. My brain didn't process this. I was so confused. I didn't know much about her faith but I knew she had more than me. Why did she need me? What could I possibly offer?

We spent the next few weeks talking for about one to two hours almost daily. I got to know my sister. I found out that she was relatively new in the faith herself. I found this hard to believe. My sister had moved to Georgia with her husband and kids years prior. While she was living there it was rough on her. She was so far away from her family and it was too expensive to talk often. She was trying to raise her kids while living with her in-laws. The stress was pretty high.

I knew she desperately wanted to move back to Delaware, but I thought this was crazy. I told her to think about it carefully. Was there work to come to? Where were they going to live? Who was going to take care of them in the meantime? I couldn't see it at the time but she was coming home, and my opinion didn't matter. God would take care of her and her family. The same God that helps those that help themselves? I still was not on the other side of this problem.

Anyway, with that kind of faith she must be convinced. She made the move within three days of making the decision. She was in Delaware before I even knew she had made up her mind. She was living with friends for the time being and her husband was looking for work. Not only did he find work, but his new boss knew of their living conditions and suggested that he buy a house for them to rent. A job and a home? No problem.

I know for a fact that I would never had made this decision and trusted God to get me through. I know for a fact that no matter what I have been through, I can't trust anyone that much. I know for a fact that my sister is crazy and reckless and she has three kids depending on her. I know this is the most irresponsible thing my sister has ever done. I don't know anything, but we'll get to that later.

I had watched everything work out for them and still I didn't believe. All I could see was all the work they had done to get here. I was glad, though, that they were here because I had missed my sister. We had been so close and I took that for granted until they moved to Georgia. Now they were back and I wouldn't take it for granted again.

We talked on the phone for a few weeks about all we had learned. I found it so easy to talk to her. I was so happy to have someone to talk to while Karl was at work. I had church on Sunday, Bible study on Saturday, prayer journal every morning, Joyce Meyer every weekday morning, my sister during the day and Karl at night. I was learning, and I was exercising what I learned. I had input coming from all directions. I had a new friend in the faith because I couldn't find Joyce Meyer on the television.

No one can do it for you

*I*t then dawned on me that in my prayer journal I had been praying for knowledge, understanding and wisdom. This God that doesn't answer my prayers is improving his track record. Not only is he answering some of my prayers, he is sending me help that I didn't even know to ask for. I can look back and see a church that is perfect for Karl and I. Glen and Roe coming into our lives. Karl getting saved. Joyce Meyer coming into our lives. And, finally, having Bridget as my new personal Bible-study partner.

Why did I feel like something was missing? I was starting to get excited about God, but something was missing. I still didn't feel like I was getting enough. I still felt like I was so far behind and there was still so much catching up to do. Maybe I should stop praying for knowledge, understanding and wisdom. I knew that this was the problem. I was now starting to look back and see that I had learned so much in four months, but it still wasn't enough for me. I needed more.

I went to the Christian store but I didn't know what to buy. I was completely lost in there. I knew I needed something else to study, but I didn't know where to begin. I was dying for the next little tidbit I would get, but where? I didn't want to complain to God because I could see how much he had already done. I didn't want to seem ungrateful.

Right in the middle of this frustration, God actually gave me a thought: "You could open the Bible yourself and learn all you want." Oh, you have got to be kidding me. That was the most confusing book I had ever seen. Talk about not knowing where to begin. I knew people that could hear a scripture and know

right where to find it in the Bible. He said, "You could do that."
Yeah, right! I still have tabs in my Bible so that I can find the
various books when I need them. I was actually sitting there
looking at my Bible like it was written in a foreign language. The
thing is, I really wanted to be able to quote scripture. I would
love to be able to do that. I know that is what real Christians
can do.

Okay, but I still don't know where to begin. The first time I
tried to read the Bible, I decided to start at the beginning and
read straight through. I made it to 2 Kings. Considering I was
convinced that God didn't like me because he was mad at me,
this wasn't the most encouraging place for me to start.

Our pastor had suggested that we start at Matthew and read
through John. We had done that a few months earlier but I didn't
really get anything new out of it. I already knew most of those
stories. I wanted something new, something I could get my head
around. While I was sitting there staring at my Bible, I happened to have some scripture references sitting around that we
had been working on in church.

I ended up in Ezekiel 37:1-14.

Ezekiel 37:1-14 (NLT)

*The Lord took hold of me, and I was carried away by
the Spirit of the Lord to a valley filled with bones. ²He led
me around among the old, dry bones that covered the valley floor. They were scattered everywhere across the ground.
³Then he asked me, "Son of man, can these bones become
living people again?"*

*"O Sovereign Lord," I replied, "you alone know the
answer to that."*

*⁴Then he said to me, "Speak to these bones and say,
'Dry bones, listen to the word of the Lord! ⁵This is what the
Sovereign Lord says: Look! I am going to breathe into you
and make you live again! ⁶I will put flesh and muscles on
you and cover you with skin. I will put breath into you, and*

you will come to life. Then you will know that I am the LORD.' "

⁷*So I spoke these words, just as he told me. Suddenly as I spoke, there was a rattling noise all across the valley. The bones of each body came together and attached themselves as they had been before.* ⁸*Then as I watched, muscles and flesh formed over the bones. Then skin formed to cover their bodies, but they still had no breath in them.*

⁹*Then he said to me, "Speak to the winds and say: 'This is what the Sovereign* LORD *says: Come, O breath, from the four winds! Breathe into these dead bodies so that they may live again.' "*

¹⁰*So I spoke as he commanded me, and the wind entered the bodies, and they began to breathe. They all came to life and stood up on their feet—a great army of them.*

¹¹*Then he said to me, "Son of man, these bones represent the people of Israel. They are saying, 'We have become old, dry bones—all hope is gone.'* ¹²*Now give them this message from the Sovereign* LORD: *O my people, I will open your graves of exile and cause you to rise again. Then I will bring you back to the land of Israel.* ¹³*When this happens, O my people, you will know that I am the* LORD. ¹⁴*I will put my Spirit in you, and you will live and return home to your own land. Then you will know that I am the* LORD. *You will see that I have done everything just as I promised. I, the* LORD, *have spoken!"*

37:1ff This vision illustrates the promise of Ezekiel 36— new life and a nation restored, both physically and spiritually. The dry bones are a picture of the Jews in captivity—scattered and dead. The two sticks (Ezekiel 37:15-17) represent the reunion of the entire nation of Israel that had divided into northern and southern kingdoms after Solomon. The scattered exiles of both Israel and Judah would be released from the "graves" of captivity and one day regathered in their homeland, with the Messiah as their leader. This vi-

sion has yet to be fulfilled. Ezekiel felt he was speaking to the dead as he preached to the exiles because they rarely responded to his message. But these bones responded! And just as God brought life to the dead bones, he would bring life again to his spiritually dead people.

37:4-5 *The dry bones represented the people's spiritually dead condition. Your church may seem like a heap of dry bones to you, spiritually dead with no hope of vitality. But just as God promised to restore his nation, he can restore any church, no matter how dry or dead it may be. Rather than give up, pray for renewal, for God can restore it to life. The hope and prayer of every church should be that God will put his Spirit into it (Ezekiel 37:14). In fact, God is at work calling his people back to himself, bringing new life into dead churches.*

I use the *New Living Translation Life Application Bible.* The references below the scripture are the notes that are contained in that Bible just as they appear. I read the scripture and the reference notes. I sat thinking. I don't know what I was looking for but I read it again. Then all of a sudden it hit me. I mean it actually hit me.

I'll walk you through my thinking. I understand that God was performing a miracle. I understand the Jews in captivity will be coming home. I had read the Old Testament and remembered the stories of Israel and Judah being taken into captivity. I understand the church being restored. In my opinion the church included anyone who went to church on Sunday. The same church where I was trying to find my place.

Then all of a sudden, my mind saw something else. The only way I can describe it is to describe those holographic pictures that used to hang in the mall. I loved those pictures. Everyone would walk up to the "picture store" in the mall and stand there staring at these pictures. Nobody could tell you how to see the

27

3D picture behind the wild-looking abstract. All they could tell you to do was, "Relax your eyes. Do not try to control your eyes and it will appear." What in God's name is that supposed to mean?

So I stood there like all the rest, and just about the time that I was getting sick of looking for it, there it was. I could see the 3D image in the picture. I tried to control my eyes and lost it, so I relaxed and there it was again. I was so excited because not everyone could see it but I could. I received one as a gift that Christmas.

Anyway, this was exactly the same thing. All of a sudden I knew that church meant every living human being. I don't know how I knew it, but it was the truth. God looks at every human being as his children even if they don't believe. *All* people are the church. God loves *all* people. God wants *all* people to come back to him. Not all will come back to him, but that doesn't change the fact that **GOD WANTS ALL**. I am part of *all*! I am *wanted* by God! And so is every human being! Just in case you don't see this, you are part of *all*. You are *wanted*!

Where he says, " *²He led me around among the old, dry bones that covered the valley floor. They were scattered everywhere across the ground.* "I could see that this didn't mean physical dead people in a heap. He was talking about physical, living people all over the earth. What these physical, living people didn't know is that they were spiritually dead. They didn't know God. God was a part of their lives but they didn't know or they didn't accept that this was true.

Where he says, *"³Then he asked me, 'Son of man, can these bones become living people again?' 'O Sovereign LORD,' I replied, 'you alone know the answer to that.'"* This actually represents me and anyone else that doubts. A dead person is a dead person, period. If a person can be raised from the dead, the only one who can raise the dead is God. How does God raise a dead person? He answers a prayer and helps you look for and find Him. He works in the lives of the people who have searched for Him. He has helpers in the way of living proof!

Where it says, *"Speak to these bones and say, 'Dry bones, listen to the word of the LORD! ⁵This is what the Sovereign LORD says: Look! I am going to breathe into you and make you live again! ⁶I will put flesh and muscles on you and cover you with skin. I will put breath into you, and you will come to life. Then you will know that I am the LORD,'"* God is talking about anyone who already knows him even in the smallest way. Tell the people about what God has done in their lives, and if and when they see and believe, their lives will be new. He will restore their lives and it will be better than before they were lost. It will be forever!

Anyone who understands even the smallest part of God should tell others so they might know him too. Why does he even want the smallest part? Because you are not the only person that will come into that person's life. He will be sending others to also speak about Him. And, maybe, just maybe, after enough people have said something, the person will finally see what you and I see. How small can it be? It can be as small as saying, "Thank God," in a situation that works out great. Or saying, "God willing," when someone asks you if you are going to do something. When someone hears you saying, "Thank God," or ,"God willing," they automatically assume you believe in God. It can be that easy!

I do that already! I have been helping God and didn't even know I was. I nearly fell off of my chair. I ran downstairs after this whole episode and told Karl. I had him read this story and then I told him what I thought. He said to me, "I never saw it that way!" I started laughing because at that moment I realized that God had just used me again. Karl asked me where I came up with my explanation of the story and I said it had to be God showing me because I am not that smart!

Deep down, I knew it was true. God had given me a free gift. He explained something to me that I could not have logically figured out by myself. There was no reason for me to read all of that into that story. I was looking. I didn't know it already when I sat down that night. Now that I understood what happened, I realized what I had found out and that it was true. ***GOD WANTS ALL, I am part of all! I am wanted by God!***

DOES GOD LOVE ME?

*T*hat started a whole new walk with God. I was so excited that He had shown me something that I was dying to know more. God basically said, "Not tonight!" Not for the next week! I couldn't believe it! I had decided to sit down with my Bible and randomly open it and read. I couldn't find anything. I wasn't seeing the 3D picture. I tried and tried and couldn't find anything.

I thought, "I've lost it." What did I do the last time to make it work? I was actually acting like this was a magic trick. I tried everything. I prayed and asked for forgiveness. Maybe if I hadn't asked for forgiveness first, it wouldn't work. I read some more. Nothing. I tried to think of everything I had done the last time to make it work. I did everything I could think of and opened the Bible. Nothing. I couldn't believe that as soon as I had gotten something and believed, that was all I was going to get. One little story to call my own.

A week later I had finally exhausted myself. I gave up! If God wanted to show me something, he was going to have to drop it in my lap. I am not looking anymore! I can't take this. I am convinced that I have lost the recipe for the trick. I will be telling you about God's patience in a little while.

Just then, God says, "Liz, what do you want to know?" I want to know everything. God says, "Liz, what do you want to know?" I want to know if I am a Christian. God says, "Liz, what do you want to know?" Everyone keeps telling me that you love me. I want to know if you really love me. I want to know that it's not too late.

I will admit that I am crying when I write this. I did not really realize that I never knew that God loved me until that moment. The things in my heart were: God is mad at me, I will be lucky if he takes me back, he probably won't take me back. How could he? I have to be perfect. I've made too many horrible mistakes, said too many things to too many people, gotten too far away from him.

It was like he was talking to me. He said, "Do you remember the 'Index to Notes' and the 'Dictionary/Concordance' in the back of the Bible?" I turned there and He said, "start with Love." This starts my "Love walk" with God. I got out my notebook. I didn't want to miss or forget a single detail about what he was going to teach me. I wrote every word of every scripture reference down in longhand. Then when I was finished, I typed the notes on my computer with all of the Bible notes. I wanted to be able to pull it out later and have it all right in front of me without flipping through the Bible.

I have those very notes in front of me as I write this.

Exodus 20:20 (NLT)

"Don't be afraid," Moses said, "for God has come in this way to show you his awesome power. From now on, let your fear of him keep you from sinning!"

20:20 *Throughout the Bible we find this phrase, "Do not be afraid." God wasn't trying to scare the people. He was showing his mighty power so the Israelites would know he was the true God and would therefore obey him. If they would do this, he would make his power available to them. God wants us to follow him out of love rather than fear. To overcome fear, we must think more about his love. 1 John 4:18 says, "Perfect love drives out fear."*

John 13:34-35 (NLT)

So now I am giving you a new commandment: Love each other. Just as I have loved you, you should love each other.

[35]*Your love for one another will prove to the world that you are my disciples."*

13:34 *To love others was not a new commandment (see Leviticus 19:18), but to love others as much as Christ loved others was revolutionary. Now we are to love others based on Jesus' sacrificial love for us. Such love will not only bring unbelievers to Christ; it will also keep believers strong and united in a world hostile to God. Jesus was a living example of God's love, as we are to be living examples of Jesus' love.*

13:34-35 *Jesus says that our Christlike love will show we are his disciples. Do people see petty bickering, jealousy, and division in your church? Or do they know you are Jesus' followers by your love for one another?*

13:35 *Love is more than simply warm feelings; it is an attitude that reveals itself in action. How can we love others as Jesus loves us? By helping when it's not convenient, by giving when it hurts, by devoting energy to others' welfare rather than our own, by absorbing hurts from others without complaining or fighting back. This kind of loving is hard to do. That is why people notice when you do it and know you are empowered by a supernatural source. The Bible has another beautiful description of love in 1 Cor. 13.*

1 Cor. 13:4-7 (NLT)

Love is patient and kind. Love is not jealous or boastful or proud [5]or rude. Love does not demand its own way. Love is not irritable, and it keeps no record of when it has been wronged. [6]It is never glad about injustice but rejoices whenever the truth wins out. [7]Love never gives up, never loses faith, is always hopeful, and endures through every circumstance.

13:4-7 Our society confuses love and lust. Unlike lust, God's kind of love is directed outward toward others, not inward toward ourselves. It is utterly unselfish. This kind of love goes against our natural inclinations. It is possible to practice this love only if God helps us set aside our own desires and instincts, so that we can give love while expecting nothing in return. Thus the more we become like Christ, the more love we will show to others.

Matthew 5:43-44 (NLT)
"You have heard that the law of Moses says, 'Love your neighbor' and hate your enemy. ⁴⁴But I say, love your enemies! Pray for those who persecute you!

5:39-44 To many Jews of Jesus' day, these statements were offensive. Any Messiah who would turn the other cheek was not the military leader they wanted to lead a revolt against Rome. Since they were under Roman oppression, they wanted retaliation against their enemies, whom they hated. But Jesus suggested a new, radical response to injustice: instead of demanding rights, give them up freely! According to Jesus, it is more important to give justice and mercy than to receive it.

5:43-44 By telling us not to retaliate, Jesus keeps us from taking the law into our own hands. By loving and praying for our enemies, we can overcome evil with good.

The Pharisees interpreted Leviticus 19:18 as teaching that they should love only those who love in return, and Psalm 139:19-22 and Psalm 140:9-11 as meaning that they should hate their enemies. But Jesus says we are to love our enemies. If you love your enemies and treat them well, you will truly show that Jesus is Lord of your life. This is possible only for those who give themselves fully to God, because only he can deliver people from natural selfish-

ness. We must trust the Holy Spirit to help us show love to those for whom we may not feel love.

Matthew 10:29-31 (NLT)

Not even a sparrow, worth only half a penny, can fall to the ground without your Father knowing it. [30]And the very hairs on your head are all numbered. [31]So don't be afraid; you are more valuable to him than a whole flock of sparrows.

10:29-31 *Jesus said that God is aware of everything that happens even to sparrows, and you are far more valuable to him than they are. You are so valuable that God sent his only Son to die for you (John 3:16). Because God places such value on you, you need never fear personal threats or difficult trials. These can't shake God's love or dislodge his Spirit from within you.*

But this doesn't mean that God will take away all your troubles (see Matthew 10:16). The real test of value is how well something holds up under the wear, tear, and abuse of everyday life. Those who stand up for Christ in spite of their troubles truly have lasting value and will receive great rewards (see Matthew 5:11-12).

Romans 8:35-39 (NLT)

Can anything ever separate us from Christ's love? Does it mean he no longer loves us if we have trouble or calamity, or are persecuted, or are hungry or cold or in danger or threatened with death? [36](Even the Scriptures say, "For your sake we are killed every day; we are being slaughtered like sheep.") [37]No, despite all these things, overwhelming victory is ours through Christ, who loved us.

[38]And I am convinced that nothing can ever separate us from his love. Death can't, and life can't. The angels can't, and the demons can't. Our fears for today, our worries about

tomorrow, and even the powers of hell can't keep God's love away. ³⁹Whether we are high above the sky or in the deepest ocean, nothing in all creation will ever be able to separate us from the love of God that is revealed in Christ Jesus our Lord.

8:35-39 *These verses contain one of the most comforting promises in all Scripture. Believers have always had to face hardships in many forms: persecution, illness, imprisonment, even death. These could cause them to fear that they have been abandoned by Christ. But Paul exclaims that it is impossible to be separated from Christ. His death for us is proof of his unconquerable love. Nothing can stop Christ's constant presence with us. God tells us how great his love is so that we will feel totally secure in him. If we believe these overwhelming assurances, we will not be afraid.*

Matthew 10:42 (NLT)
And if you give even a cup of cold water to one of the least of my followers, you will surely be rewarded."

10:42 *How much we love God can be measured by how well we treat others. Jesus' example of giving a cup of cold water to a thirsty child is a good model of unselfish service. A child usually can't or won't return a favor. God notices every good deed we do or don't do as if he were the one receiving it. Is there something unselfish you can do for someone else today? Although no one else may see you, God will notice.*

Mark 12:29-31 (NLT)
Jesus replied, "The most important commandment is this: 'Hear, O Israel! The Lord our God is the one and only Lord. ³⁰And you must love the Lord your God with all your heart,

all your soul, all your mind, and all your strength.' ³¹*The
second is equally important: 'Love your neighbor as yourself.' No other commandment is greater than these."*

12:29-31 *God's laws are not burdensome. They can be
reduced to two simple principles: love God and love others.
These commands are from the Old Testament (Deut. 6:5;
Leviticus 19:18). When you love God completely and care
for others as you care for yourself, then you have fulfilled
the intent of the Ten Commandments and the other Old
Testament laws. According to Jesus, these two commandments summarize all God's laws. Let them rule your
thoughts, decisions, and actions. When you are uncertain
about what to do, ask yourself which course of action best
demonstrates love for God and love for others.*

Acts 2:47 (NLT)
*all the while praising God and enjoying the goodwill of
all the people. And each day the Lord added to their group
those who were being saved.*

2:47 *A healthy Christian community attracts people to
Christ. The Jerusalem church's zeal for worship and broth-
erly love was contagious. A healthy, loving church will grow
in numbers. What are you doing to make your church the
kind of place that will attract others to Christ?*

Romans 5:2-5 (NLT)
*Because of our faith, Christ has brought us into this place
of highest privilege where we now stand, and we confidently
and joyfully look forward to sharing God's glory.*
*³We can rejoice, too, when we run into problems and
trials, for we know that they are good for us—they help us
learn to endure. ⁴And endurance develops strength of character in us, and character strengthens our confident*

expectation of salvation. ⁵And this expectation will not dis-appoint us. For we know how dearly God loves us, because he has given us the Holy Spirit to fill our hearts with his love.

5:2 *Paul states that, as believers, we now stand in a place of highest privilege ("this grace in which we now stand"). Not only has God declared us not guilty; he has drawn us close to himself. Instead of being enemies, we have become his friends—in fact, his own children (John 15:15; Galatians 4:5).*

5:2-5 *As Paul states clearly in 1 Cor. 13:13, faith, hope, and love are at the heart of the Christian life. Our relation-ship with God begins with faith, which helps us realize that we are delivered from our past by Christ's death. Hope grows as we learn all that God has in mind for us; it gives us the promise of the future. And God's love fills our lives and gives us the ability to reach out to others.*

5:3-4 *For first-century Christians, suffering was the rule rather than the exception. Paul tells us that in the future we will become, but until then we must overcome. This means we will experience difficulties that help us grow. We rejoice in suffering not because we like pain or deny its tragedy, but because we know God is using life's difficulties and Satan's attacks to build our character. The problems that we run into will develop our perse-verance—which in turn will strengthen our character, deepen our trust in God, and give us greater confidence about the future. You probably find your patience tested in some way every day. Thank God for those opportuni-ties to grow, and deal with them in his strength (see also James 1:2-4; 1 Peter 1:6-7).*

Romans 12:9 (NLT)
Don't just pretend that you love others. Really love them. Hate what is wrong. Stand on the side of the good.

12:9 Most of us have learned how to pretend to love others—how to speak kindly, avoid hurting their feelings, and appear to take an interest in them. We may even be skilled in pretending to feel moved with compassion when we hear of others' needs, or to become indignant when we learn of injustice. But God calls us to real and sincere love that goes far beyond pretense and politeness. Sincere love requires concentration and effort. It means helping others become better people. It demands our time, money, and personal involvement. No individual has the capacity to express love to a whole community, but the body of Christ in your town does. Look for people who need your love, and look for ways you and your fellow believers can love your community for Christ.

Romans 13:8 (NLT)
Pay all your debts, except the debt of love for others. You can never finish paying that! If you love your neighbor, you will fulfill all the requirements of God's law.

13:8 Why is love for others called a debt? We are permanently in debt to Christ for the lavish love he has poured out on us. The only way we can even begin to repay this debt is by loving others in turn. Because Christ's love will always be infinitely greater than ours, we will always have the obligation to love our neighbors.

Romans 13:10 (NLT)
Love does no wrong to anyone, so love satisfies all of God's requirements.

Liz Kraus

13:10 *Christians must obey the law of love, which supersedes both religious and civil laws. How easy it is to excuse our indifference to others merely because we have no legal obligation to help them, and even to justify harming them if our actions are technically legal! But Jesus does not leave loopholes in the law of love. Whenever love demands it, we are to go beyond human legal requirements and imitate the God of love. See James 2:8-9; James 4:11 and 1 Peter 2:16-17 for more about this law of love.*

Galatians 5:14-15 (NLT)
For the whole law can be summed up in this one command: "Love your neighbor as yourself." ¹⁵But if instead of showing love among yourselves you are always biting and devouring one another, watch out! Beware of destroying one another.

5:14-15 *When we are not motivated by love, we become critical of others. We stop looking for good in them and see only their faults. Soon the unity of believers is broken. Have you talked behind someone's back? Have you focused on others' shortcomings instead of their strengths? Remind yourself of Jesus' command to love others as you love yourself (Matthew 22:39). When you begin to feel critical of someone, make a list of that person's positive qualities. If there are problems that need to be addressed, it is better to confront in love than to gossip.*

Ephes. 3:17-19 (NLT)
And I pray that Christ will be more and more at home in your hearts as you trust in him. May your roots go down deep into the soil of God's marvelous love. ¹⁸And may you have the power to understand, as all God's people should, how wide, how long, how high, and how deep his love really is. ¹⁹May you experience the love of Christ, though it is

40

so great you will never fully understand it. Then you will be filled with the fullness of life and power that comes from God.

3:17-19 *God's love is total, says Paul. It reaches every corner of our experience. It is wide—it covers the breadth of our own experience, and it reaches out to the whole world. God's love is long—it continues the length of our lives. It is high—it rises to the heights of our celebration and elation. His love is deep—it reaches to the depths of discouragement, despair, and even death. When you feel shut out or isolated, remember that you can never be lost to God's love. For another prayer about God's immeasurable and inexhaustible love, see Paul's words in Romans 8:38-39.*

Hebrews 12:5-11 (NLT)
And have you entirely forgotten the encouraging words God spoke to you, his children? He said,

> *"My child, don't ignore it when the Lord disciplines you,*
> *and don't be discouraged when he corrects you.*
> *⁶For the Lord disciplines those he loves,*
> *and he punishes those he accepts as his children."*

⁷As you endure this divine discipline, remember that God is treating you as his own children. Whoever heard of a child who was never disciplined? ⁸If God doesn't discipline you as he does all of his children, it means that you are illegitimate and are not really his children after all. ⁹Since we respect our earthly fathers who disciplined us, should we not all the more cheerfully submit to the discipline of our heavenly Father and live forever?

¹⁰For our earthly fathers disciplined us for a few years, doing the best they knew how. But God's discipline is always right and good for us because it means we will share in his holiness. [11]*No discipline is enjoyable while it is happening—it is painful! But afterward there will be a quiet harvest of right living for those who are trained in this way.*

12:5-11 Who loves his child more—the father who allows the child to do what will harm him, or the one who corrects, trains, and even punishes the child to help him learn what is right? It's never pleasant to be corrected and disciplined by God, but his discipline is a sign of his deep love for us. When God corrects you, see it as proof of his love and ask him what he is trying to teach you.

Hebrews 13:1-5 (NLT)

Continue to love each other with true Christian love. [2]*Don't forget to show hospitality to strangers, for some who have done this have entertained angels without realizing it!* [3]*Don't forget about those in prison. Suffer with them as though you were there yourself. Share the sorrow of those being mistreated, as though you feel their pain in your own bodies.*

[4]*Give honor to marriage, and remain faithful to one another in marriage. God will surely judge people who are immoral and those who commit adultery.*

[5]*Stay away from the love of money; be satisfied with what you have. For God has said,*

"I will never fail you.
I will never forsake you."

13:1-5 Real love for others produces tangible actions: (1) kindness to strangers (Hebrews 13:2); (2) empathy for those who are in prison and those who have been mistreated (Hebrews 13:3); (3) respect for your marriage vows (Hebrews 13:4); and (4) contentment with what you have (Hebrews 13:5). Make sure that your love runs deep enough to affect your hospitality, empathy, fidelity, and content-ment.

13:2 Three Old Testament people "entertained angels without knowing it": (1) Abraham (Genesis 18:1ff), (2) Gideon (Judges 6:11ff), and (3) Manoah (Judges 13:2ff). Some people say they cannot be hospitable because their homes are not large enough or nice enough. But even if you have no more than a table and two chairs in a rented room, there are people who would be grateful to spend time in your home. Are there visitors to your church with whom you could share a meal? Do you know single people who would enjoy an evening of conversation? Is there any way your home could meet the needs of traveling missionaries? Hospitality simply means making other people feel com-fortable and at home.

13:3 We are to have empathy for those in prison, espe-cially for (but not limited to) Christians imprisoned for their faith. Jesus said that his true followers would represent him as they visit those in prison (Matthew 25:36).

13:5 How can we learn to be content? Strive to live with less rather than desiring more; give away out of your abun-dance rather than accumulating more; relish what you have rather than resent what you're missing. See God's love ex-pressed in what he has provided, and remember that money and possessions will all pass away. (See Phil. 4:11 for more on contentment, and 1 John 2:17 for the futility of earthly desires.)

13:5-6 We become content when we realize God's suffi-ciency for our needs. Christians who become materialistic are saying by their actions that God can't take care of them—or at least that he won't take care of them the way

43

they want. Insecurity can lead to the love of money, whether we are rich or poor. The only antidote is to trust God to meet all our needs.

1 John 2:9-11 (NLT)

If anyone says, "I am living in the light," but hates a Christian brother or sister, that person is still living in darkness. ¹⁰Anyone who loves other Christians is living in the light and does not cause anyone to stumble. ¹¹Anyone who hates a Christian brother or sister is living and walking in darkness. Such a person is lost, having been blinded by the darkness.

2:9-11 Does this mean that if you dislike someone you aren't a Christian? These verses are not talking about disliking a disagreeable Christian brother or sister. There will always be people we will not like as well as others. John's words focus on the attitude that causes us to ignore or despise others, to treat them as irritants, competitors, or enemies. Christian love is not a feeling but a choice. We can choose to be concerned with people's well-being and treat them with respect, whether or not we feel affection toward them. If we choose to love others, God will help us express our love.

1 John 4:8 (NLT)

But anyone who does not love does not know God—for God is love.

4:8 John says, "God is love," not "Love is God." Our world, with its shallow and selfish view of love, has turned these words around and contaminated our understanding of love. The world thinks that love is what makes a person feel good and that it is all right to sacrifice moral principles and others' rights in order to obtain such "love." But that *isn't real love; it is the exact opposite—selfishness. And God is not that kind of "love." Real love is like God, who is holy, just, and perfect. If we truly know God, we will love as he does.*

1 John 4:9-10 (NLT)
God showed how much he loved us by sending his only Son into the world so that we might have eternal life through him. [10]This is real love. It is not that we loved God, but that he loved us and sent his Son as a sacrifice to take away our sins.

4:9 Jesus is God's only Son. While all believers are sons and daughters of God, only Jesus lives in this special unique relationship (see John 1:18; John 3:16).

4:9-10 Love explains (1) why God creates—because he loves, he creates people to love; (2) why God cares—because he loves them, he cares for sinful people; (3) why we are free to choose—God wants a loving response from us; (4) why Christ died—his love for us caused him to seek a solution to the problem of sin; and (5) why we receive eternal life—God's love expresses itself to us forever.

4:10 Nothing sinful or evil can exist in God's presence. He is absolute goodness. He cannot overlook, condone, or excuse sin as though it never happened. He loves us, but his love does not make him morally lax. If we trust in Christ, however, we will not have to bear the penalty for our sins (1 Peter 2:24). We will be acquitted (Romans 5:18) by his atoning sacrifice.

1 John 4:19 (NLT)
We love each other as a result of his loving us first.

4:19 God's love is the source of all human love, and it spreads like fire. In loving his children, God kindles a flame in their hearts. In turn, they love others, who are warmed by God's love through them.

I haven't included all of my notes, but as you can see, there are many. I found myself re-reading certain ones over and over. Not just the scriptures but the notes as well. They also helped me look at the scriptures a different way. I started to look for the proof that I was loved. Many of the scriptures talk about certain people being loved. I wanted to know how I could be included in this group.

I took a closer look at John 13:34-35. It says, *"Your love for one another will **prove** to the world that you are my disciples."* I can do that. With some people, I already am doing that. Loving someone else seems easy. I love many different people for many different reasons. I am already proving to the world that I am a disciple.

I especially liked Matthew 10:29-31. It says, *"So don't be afraid; you are more valuable to him than a whole flock of sparrows."* That's right, God made everything and he cares for everything he made. He made me and I am more valuable to him than a whole flock of sparrows. I found myself repeating that one over the next couple of weeks to remind myself.

The next one that really caught my eye was Romans 8:35-39. I was a person who definitely needed to know the answer to the question asked. *"Can anything ever separate us from Christ's love?"* I still hold onto this one. Christ loves me in spite of me. It doesn't matter how I feel about it, he loves me anyway. He gave up his life for **me**.

Then I got down to Ephesians 3:17-19 and it hit me like a ton of bricks. *"And may you have the power to understand, as all God's people should, how wide, how long, how high, and how deep his love really is."* I'm starting to really understand. He doesn't love like a human. He is not limited to human emotions. His love is complete, perfect, and never-ending.

By the time I got to 1 John 4:8 I was starting to see the pattern. *". . . for God is love."* And then in 1 John 4:9-10, *"It is not that we loved God, but that he loved us."* And finally in 1 John 4:19, *"We love each other as a result of his loving us first."* It started to occur to me that we wouldn't even be able to love without God. Why do I even have the nerve to believe that I can out-love God? Was that what I was thinking? I guess it was. It seems so arrogant of me now but I didn't know all of this until I did the study.

I had all the proof I needed that God did indeed love me. I was worthy of his love. Not because of something I did, but because of something he did. He created me! To not love me would be to say that he made a mistake. Just in case you're wondering, God doesn't make mistakes. Only people do, and I don't want to make them anymore. I want him to be proud of me.

I hope you will pray about and meditate on the scriptures I have given you. I hope you will go on your own search. No one should wonder. No one has to wonder. All the answers are in the Bible. All you need to do is find them and have God show you. Shortly after I did this study, I happened to be in my bedroom thinking about what I had learned. I was curling my hair, so I had nothing better to do than think.

All of a sudden . . . Oh no, here she goes again. I don't have a better way of explaining it, I'm sorry. Anyway, God asked me, "What would happen if someone came to your door and told you that he didn't think you were doing a good job as a mother. Not only that, but your kids heard this person and agreed with them." This person said, "I am taking your kids and I will do a better job with them and they will enjoy themselves." Your kids again agreed and left with them.

God said, "How would you feel?" The first emotion was anger. Okay, rage. I'm going to kill this person. God said, "How do you feel about your kids?" Hurt, destroyed, deeply sad.

God said, "What would you do if your kids came back and said they were sorry?" Take them back, of course. They are my kids. God said, "You have just been put in my shoes."

I almost burned myself with the curling iron. I started laughing, it just bubbled up inside me. I couldn't help myself. Coming back and saying I was sorry was good enough for him. He loved me. Really loved me! I may have gone off like a rebellious teenager for a while, but the point was that I had come back. I wanted to come back and he knew I was serious. I was really sorry and that was all he needed. Not only that but the best was yet to come. He wasn't even going to remember this little episode. He was going to forget all about it and forgive me!

Now I know what love is! Now I know that he loves me! Now I know that I love him! All I want to do now is whatever he wants me to do. I do not ever want to do anything to lose that kind of love. How do I know what to do? Go to the Bible.

OKAY, GOD LOVES ME, BUT AM I SAVED?

*T*he next study I did was a study on salvation. I knew God loved me and I just wanted to make sure that I was still saved. I wasn't sure if there was something else I had to do. Was I still saved from 1984? Did I have to do it all over again? I would. I knew that I would. Let's see what the Bible says.

Luke 24:47 (NLT)
With my authority, take this message of repentance to all the nations, beginning in Jerusalem: 'There is forgiveness of sins for all who turn to me.'

24:47 *Luke wrote to the Greek-speaking world. He wanted them to know that Christ's message of God's love and forgiveness should go to all the world. We must never ignore the worldwide scope of Christ's gospel. God wants all the world to hear the Good News of salvation.*

Matthew 1:20-23 (NLT)
As he considered this, he fell asleep, and an angel of the Lord appeared to him in a dream. "Joseph, son of David," the angel said, "do not be afraid to go ahead with your marriage to Mary. For the child within her has been conceived by the Holy Spirit. [21]And she will have a son, and you are to name him Jesus, for he will save his people from their sins." [22]All of this happened to fulfill the Lord's message through his prophet:

²³"Look! The virgin will conceive a child!
She will give birth to a son,
and he will be called Immanuel
(meaning, God is with us)."

1:20-23 *The angel declared to Joseph that Mary's child was conceived by the Holy Spirit and would be a son. This reveals an important truth about Jesus—he is both God and human. The infinite, unlimited God took on the limitations of humanity so he could live and die for the salvation of all who would believe in him.*

1:21 *Jesus means "the LORD saves." Jesus came to earth to save us because we can't save ourselves from sin and its consequences. No matter how good we are, we can't eliminate the sinful nature present in all of us. Only Jesus can do that. Jesus didn't come to help people save themselves; he came to be their Savior from the power and penalty of sin. Thank Christ for his death on the cross for your sin, and then ask him to take control of your life. Your new life begins at that moment.*

Matthew 7:13-14 (NLT)
"You can enter God's Kingdom only through the narrow gate. The highway to hell is broad, and its gate is wide for the many who choose the easy way. ¹⁴But the gateway to life is small, and the road is narrow, and only a few ever find it.

7:13-14 *The gate that leads to eternal life (John 10:7-9) is called "narrow." This does not mean that it is difficult to become a Christian, but that there is only one way to live eternally with God and only a few that decide to walk that road. Believing in Jesus is the only way to heaven, because he alone died for our sins and made us right before God.*

Living his way may not be popular, but it is true and right. Thank God there is one way!

Acts 4:12 (NLT)
There is salvation in no one else! There is no other name in all of heaven for people to call on to save them."

4:12 Many people react negatively to the fact that there is no other name than that of Jesus to call on for salvation. Yet this is not something the church decided; it is the specific teaching of Jesus himself (John 14:6). If God designated Jesus to be the Savior of the world, no one else can be his equal. Christians are to be open-minded on many issues, but not on how we are saved from sin. No other religious teacher could die for our sins; no other religious teacher came to earth as God's only Son; no other religious teacher rose from the dead. Our focus should be on Jesus, whom God offered as the way to have an eternal relationship with himself. There is no other name or way!

Romans 2:1 (NLT)
You may be saying, "What terrible people you have been talking about!" But you are just as bad, and you have no excuse! When you say they are wicked and should be punished, you are condemning yourself, for you do these very same things.

2:1 When Paul's letter was read in the Roman church, no doubt many heads nodded as he condemned idol worshipers, homosexual practices, and violent people. But what surprise his listeners must have felt when he turned on them and said in effect, "You have no excuse. You are just as bad!" Paul was emphatically stressing that nobody is good enough to save himself or herself. If we want to avoid pun-

ishment and live eternally with Christ, all of us, whether we have been murderers and molesters or whether we have been honest, hard-working, solid citizens, must depend totally on God's grace. Paul is not discussing whether some sins are worse than others. Any sin is enough to lead us to depend on Jesus Christ for salvation and eternal life. We have all sinned repeatedly, and there is no way apart from Christ to be saved from sin's consequences.

Mark 3:11 (NLT)
And whenever those possessed by evil spirits caught sight of him, they would fall down in front of him shrieking, "You are the Son of God!"

3:11 The evil spirits knew that Jesus was the Son of God, but they refused to turn from their evil purposes. Knowing about Jesus, or even believing that he is God's Son, does not guarantee salvation. You must also want to follow and obey him (see also James 2:17).

Luke 1:30-31 (NLT)
"Don't be frightened, Mary," the angel told her, "for God has decided to bless you! [31] You will become pregnant and have a son, and you are to name him Jesus.

1:30-31 God's favor does not automatically bring instant success or fame. His blessing on Mary, the honor of being the mother of the Messiah, would lead to much pain: her peers would ridicule her; her fiance would come close to leaving her; her son would be rejected and murdered. But through her son would come the world's only hope, and this is why Mary has been praised by countless generations as the young girl who "found favor with God." Her submission was part of God's plan to bring about our salvation. If sorrow weighs you down and dims your hope, think of

Mary and wait patiently for God to finish working out his plan.

Luke 7:11-17 (NLT)

Soon afterward Jesus went with his disciples to the village of Nain, with a great crowd following him. [12]A funeral procession was coming out as he approached the village gate. The boy who had died was the only son of a widow, and many mourners from the village were with her. [13]When the Lord saw her, his heart overflowed with compassion. "Don't cry!" he said. [14]Then he walked over to the coffin and touched it, and the bearers stopped. "Young man," he said, "get up." [15]Then the dead boy sat up and began to talk to those around him! And Jesus gave him back to his mother.

[16]Great fear swept the crowd, and they praised God, saying, "A mighty prophet has risen among us," and "We have seen the hand of God at work today." [17]The report of what Jesus had done that day spread all over Judea and even out across its borders.

7:11-17 *This story illustrates salvation. The whole world was dead in sin (Ephes. 2:1), just as the widow's son was dead. Being dead, we could do nothing to help ourselves— we couldn't even ask for help. But God had compassion on us, and he sent Jesus to raise us to life with him (Ephes. 2:4-7). The dead man did not earn his second chance at life, and we cannot earn our new life in Christ. But we can accept God's gift of life, praise God for it, and use our lives to do his will.*

1 Cor. 1:28-31 (NLT)

God chose things despised by the world, things counted as nothing at all, and used them to bring to nothing what the world considers important, [29]so that no one can ever boast in the presence of God.

³⁰*God alone made it possible for you to be in Christ Jesus. For our benefit God made Christ to be wisdom itself. He is the one who made us acceptable to God. He made us pure and holy, and he gave himself to purchase our freedom.* ³¹*As the Scriptures say,*

"*The person who wishes to boast should boast only of what the Lord has done.*"

1:28-31 *Paul continues to emphasize that the way to receive salvation is so simple that any person who wants to can understand it. Skill and wisdom do not get a person into God's kingdom—simple faith does—so no one can boast that his or her achievements helped him or her secure eternal life. Salvation is totally from God through Jesus' death. There is nothing we can do to earn our salvation; we need only accept what Jesus has already done for us.*

Romans 10:8-12 (NLT)
Salvation that comes from trusting Christ—which is the message we preach—is already within easy reach. In fact, the Scriptures say, "The message is close at hand; it is on your lips and in your heart." ⁹*For if you confess with your mouth that Jesus is Lord and believe in your heart that God raised him from the dead, you will be saved.* ¹⁰*For it is by believing in your heart that you are made right with God, and it is by confessing with your mouth that you are saved.* ¹¹*As the Scriptures tell us, "Anyone who believes in him will not be disappointed."* ¹²*Jew and Gentile are the same in this respect. They all have the same Lord, who generously gives his riches to all who ask for them.*

10:6-8 *Paul adapts Moses' farewell challenge from Deut. 30:11-14 to apply to Christ. Christ has provided our salvation through his incarnation (coming to earth) and* resurrection (coming back from the dead). God's salvation is right in front of us. He will come to us wherever we are. All we need to do is to respond and accept his gift of salvation. The deep as used here refers to the grave or Hades, the place of the dead.

10:8-12 Have you ever been asked, "How do I become a Christian?" These verses give you the beautiful answer—salvation is as close as your own mouth and heart. People think it must be a complicated process, but it is not. If we believe in our hearts and say with our mouths that Christ is the risen Lord, we will be saved.

10:11 This verse must be read in context. Paul is not saying Christians will never be put to shame or be disappointed. There will be times when people will let us down and when circumstances will take a turn for the worse. Paul is saying that God will keep his side of the bargain—those who call on him will be saved. God will never fail to provide righteousness to those who believe.

Luke 24:51 (NLT)
While he was blessing them, he left them and was taken up to heaven.

24:50-53 As the disciples stood and watched, Jesus began rising into the air, and soon he disappeared into heaven. Seeing Jesus leave must have been frightening, but the disciples knew that Jesus would keep his promise to be with them through the Holy Spirit. This same Jesus, who lived with the disciples, who died and was buried, and who rose from the dead, loves us and promises to be with us always. We can get to know him better through studying the Scriptures, praying, and allowing the Holy Spirit to make us more like Jesus.

John 6:39 (NLT)

And this is the will of God, that I should not lose even one of all those he has given me, but that I should raise them to eternal life at the last day.

6:39 *Jesus said he would not lose even one person whom the Father had given him. Thus anyone who makes a sincere commitment to believe in Jesus Christ as Savior is secure in God's promise of eternal life. Christ will not let his people be overcome by Satan and lose their salvation (see also John 17:12; Phil. 1:6).*

1 John 2:3-6 (NLT)

And how can we be sure that we belong to him? By obeying his commandments. ⁴If someone says, "I belong to God," but doesn't obey God's commandments, that person is a liar and does not live in the truth. ⁵But those who obey God's word really do love him. That is the way to know whether or not we live in him. ⁶Those who say they live in God should live their lives as Christ did.

2:3-6 *How can you be sure that you belong to Christ? This passage gives two ways to know: if you do what Christ says and live as Christ wants. What does Christ tell us to do? John answers in 1 John 3:23: "to believe in the name of his Son, Jesus Christ, and to love one another." True Christian faith results in loving behavior; that is why John says that the way we act can give us assurance that we belong to Christ.*

John 6:44 (NLT)

For people can't come to me unless the Father who sent me draws them to me, and at the last day I will raise them from the dead.

6:44 God, not man, plays the most active role in salvation. When someone chooses to believe in Jesus Christ as Savior, he or she does so only in response to the urging of God's Holy Spirit. God does the urging; then we decide whether or not to believe. Thus no one can believe in Jesus without God's help.

Galatians 2:17-19 (NLT)
But what if we seek to be made right with God through faith in Christ and then find out that we are still sinners? Has Christ led us into sin? Of course not! ¹⁸Rather, I make myself guilty if I rebuild the old system I already tore down. ¹⁹For when I tried to keep the law, I realized I could never earn God's approval. So I died to the law so that I might live for God. I have been crucified with Christ.

2:17-19 Through studying the Old Testament Scriptures, Paul realized that he could not be saved by obeying God's laws. The prophets knew that God's plan of salvation did not rest on keeping the law (see the chart in Galatians 3:25 for references). Because we have all been infected by sin, we cannot keep God's laws perfectly. Fortunately, God has provided a way of salvation that depends on Jesus Christ, not on our own efforts. Even though we know this truth, we must guard against the temptation of using service, good deeds, charitable giving, or any other effort as a substitute for faith.

Romans 3:10-18 (NLT)
*As the Scriptures say,
"No one is good—
not even one.
¹¹No one has real understanding;
no one is seeking God.
¹²All have turned away from God;*

all have gone wrong.
No one does good,
not even one."
[13]"Their talk is foul, like the stench from an open grave.
Their speech is filled with lies."
"The poison of a deadly snake drips from their lips."
[14]"Their mouths are full of cursing and bitterness."
[15]"They are quick to commit murder.
[16]Wherever they go, destruction and misery follow them.
[17]They do not know what true peace is."
[18]"They have no fear of God to restrain them."

3:10-12 Paul is referring to Psalm 14:1-3. "There is no one righteous" means "no one is innocent." Every person is valuable in God's eyes because God created us in his image and he loves us. But no one is righteous (that is, no one can earn right standing with God). Though valuable, we have fallen into sin. But God, through Jesus his Son, has redeemed us and offers to forgive us if we return to him in faith.

3:10-18 Paul uses these Old Testament references to show that humanity in general, in its present sinful condition, is unacceptable before God. Have you ever thought to yourself, "Well, I'm not too bad. I'm a pretty good person"? Look at these verses and see if any of them apply to you. Have you ever lied? Have you ever hurt someone's feelings by your words or tone of voice? Are you bitter toward anyone? Do you become angry with those who strongly disagree with you? In thought, word, and deed you, like everyone else in the world, stand guilty before God. We must remember who we are in his sight—alienated sinners. Don't deny that you are a sinner. Instead, allow your desperate need to point you toward Christ.

Romans 3:28 (NLT)
So we are made right with God through faith and not by obeying the law.

3:27-28 *Most religions prescribe specific duties that must be performed to make a person acceptable to a god. Christianity is unique in teaching that the good deeds we do will not make us right with God. No amount of human achievement or progress in personal development will close the gap between God's moral perfection and our imperfect daily performance. Good deeds are important, but they will not earn us eternal life. We are saved only by trusting in what God has done for us (see Ephes. 2:8-10).*

3:28 *Why does God save us by faith alone? (1) Faith eliminates the pride of human effort, because faith is not a deed that we do. (2) Faith exalts what God has done, not what people do. (3) Faith admits that we can't keep the law or measure up to God's standards—we need help. (4) Faith is based on our relationship with God, not our performance for God.*

Romans 4:5 (NLT)
But people are declared righteous because of their faith, not because of their work.

4:5 *When some people learn that they are saved by God through faith, they start to worry. "Do I have enough faith?" they wonder, "Is my faith strong enough to save me?" These people miss the point. It is Jesus Christ who saves us, not our feelings or actions, and he is strong enough to save us no matter how weak our faith is. Jesus offers us salvation as a gift because he loves us, not because we have earned it through our powerful faith. What, then, is the role of faith? Faith is believing and trusting in Jesus Christ, and reaching out to accept his wonderful gift of salvation.*

Ephes. 2:8-10 (NLT)
God saved you by his special favor when you believed. And you can't take credit for this; it is a gift from God. ⁹Salvation is not a reward for the good things we have done, so none of us can boast about it. ¹⁰For we are God's masterpiece. He has created us anew in Christ Jesus, so that we can do the good things he planned for us long ago.

2:8-9 *When someone gives you a gift, do you say, "That's very nice—now how much do I owe you?" No, the appropriate response to a gift is "Thank you." Yet how often Christians, even after they have been given the gift of salvation, feel obligated to try to work their way to God. Because our salvation and even our faith are gifts, we should respond with gratitude, praise, and joy.*

2:8-10 *We become Christians through God's unmerited grace, not as the result of any effort, ability, intelligent choice, or act of service on our part. However, out of gratitude for this free gift, we will seek to help and serve others with kindness, love, and gentleness, and not merely to please ourselves. While no action or work we do can help us obtain salvation, God's intention is that our salvation will result in acts of service. We are not saved merely for our own benefit but to serve Christ and build up the church (Ephes. 4:12).*

1 Tim. 2:4 (NLT)
for he wants everyone to be saved and to understand the truth.

2:4 *Both Peter and Paul said that God wants all to be saved (see 2 Peter 3:9). This does not mean that all will be saved, because the Bible makes it clear that many reject Christ (Matthew 25:31-46; John 12:44-50; Hebrews 10:26-*

My First Year in the Lord's Family

29). The gospel message has a universal scope; it is not directed only to people of one race, one sex, or one national background. God loves the whole world and sent his Son to save sinners. Never assume that anyone is outside God's mercy or beyond the reach of his offer of salvation.

Hebrews 11:6 (NLT)
So, you see, it is impossible to please God without faith. Anyone who wants to come to him must believe that there is a God and that he rewards those who sincerely seek him.

11:6 Believing that God exists is only the beginning; even the demons believe that much (James 2:19-20). God will not settle for mere acknowledgment of his existence. He wants a personal, dynamic relationship with you that will transform your life. Those who seek God will find that they are rewarded with his intimate presence.

As I was studying these scriptures and notes on Salvation, I noticed that I could feel all of the underlying love in the scriptures. Some of the scriptures don't seem real encouraging, but I could feel the love that comes from someone who wants you to understand. God could have kept all of this secret. He could have made it difficult to get into heaven. He loves us so much that he gave us the Bible to show us the way. He clearly states over and over what we should do and what we should avoid doing. He didn't have to do that. Parents do that with their children to keep them from getting hurt. That is real love.

I took a closer look at some of the scriptures. They seemed to jump off the page to me. Matthew 7:13-14 says, *"You can enter God's Kingdom only through the narrow gate,"* and, *"only a few ever find it."* Yeah, that is what really has me worried. How do I become one of the few?

Then I read Acts 4:12 where it says, *"There is no other name in all of heaven for people to call on to save them."* I understand that Jesus is the name. I understand that people can call on him to save them. What I don't understand is how and when do you know?

I moved on to 1 Corinthians 1:28-31 and read that, *"God alone made it possible for you to be in Christ Jesus."* This is where my thinking started to turn around. Does this mean that I wasn't actively seeking God as I thought? Wasn't I the one that made the decision to start this journey? Wasn't I the one sitting on my couch calling out to God? No. It dawned on me that He had given me the idea to call out to him. I couldn't have even called out to Him without his help.

I already learned that He loved me. He had no intention of leaving me stranded. He had suggested that I call to Him for help. He had wanted to help but He couldn't do anything until I asked. He already had me handpicked *"to be in Christ Jesus."* This was an awesome thing that God had already chosen me even before I called to Him. He knew me and wanted me anyway. I am still getting proof that I am wanted.

In Romans 10:8-12 it says, *"Salvation that comes from trusting Christ—which is the message we preach—is already within easy reach."* And that is, *"For if you confess with your mouth that Jesus is Lord and believe in your heart that God raised him from the dead, you will be saved."* That's it? All I have to do is believe that Jesus is the Lord in my life and that God raised him from the dead? Done. I already believed that. How did I know that I believed that? I've been saying it all along. I had been confessing it all along!

I still looked and found some other scriptures that touched my heart. John 6:44 says, *"For people can't come to me unless the Father who sent me draws them to me."* This is saying the same thing as 1 Corinthians 1:30. I am not saved because of anything I have done. Calling out to God and believing he would be there weren't even my ideas. They were given to me as free gifts from God. Not only does he answer prayers, but he tells you what to pray for.

Then in Romans 3:28 it says, *"So we are made right with God through faith and not by obeying the law."* And again in Romans 4:5 it says, *"But people are declared righteous because of their faith, not because of their work."* I couldn't have done anything to save myself. Save myself from what? I needed to be saved from the one barrier that came between me and God. My sins! I can't go to him unless I am spotless. I have to be perfect. Have you been reading my story—I am definitely not perfect. What do I do to become perfect? I don't do anything. Jesus already did it. All I had to do was believe that what Jesus did was enough.

Let me show you two more scriptures that I really love. In 1 Timothy 2:4 it says, *"for he wants everyone to be saved and to understand the truth."* Do you remember earlier in this book when I told you what God showed me about Ezekiel 37:1-14? About God wanting all? Isn't it funny that I found this particular scripture during my salvation study? I was able to remember that revelation like I had found it yesterday. I just didn't really accept it as a revelation until the day I found this scripture.

And finally, one that is so important to me. After the life I have led, it is really important to me to do my very best to please God. I have been on the wrong side and I want to make it right. How do I do that? In Hebrews 11:6 it says, *"So, you see, it is impossible to please God without faith. Anyone who wants to come to him must believe that there is a God and that he rewards those who sincerely seek him."*

The one sticking point for me was forgiveness. I could be saved if I believed that Jesus paid the price for my sins. I wish I hadn't done so many things wrong in my life. I wish I didn't have to look back over all the years. Do I just forget? How do I forget how awful I have been? How do I believe that God won't remember any of my sins?

The next day, I was peeling a banana and it had some brown spots. I was cutting the brown spots off and I was thinking about this study. I thought if this banana represented my life, there isn't much left for God to work with. Just then God reminded me of something that I had learned in church. I went and looked it up.

John 15:1-8 (NLT)

"I am the true vine, and my Father is the gardener. ²He cuts off every branch that doesn't produce fruit, and he prunes the branches that do bear fruit so they will produce even more. ³You have already been pruned for greater fruitfulness by the message I have given you. ⁴Remain in me, and I will remain in you. For a branch cannot produce fruit if it is severed from the vine, and you cannot be fruitful apart from me.

⁵"Yes, I am the vine; you are the branches. Those who remain in me, and I in them, will produce much fruit. For apart from me you can do nothing. ⁶Anyone who parts from me is thrown away like a useless branch and withers. Such branches are gathered into a pile to be burned. ⁷But if you stay joined to me and my words remain in you, you may ask any request you like, and it will be granted! ⁸My true disciples produce much fruit. This brings great glory to my Father.

I am not the banana! I am not the fruit, I am the branch. God can grow new fruit. The old, ugly, awful fruit falls off and disappears. In its place grows new, ripe, beautiful fruit. No one remembers the rotten fruit that has disappeared. Everyone remembers the ripe fruit and how they enjoyed it. God looks at our sins in this way. He can easily forget the rotten fruit of our lives and focus on the new, beautiful, ripe fruit of our lives. He knows we are really sorry because we are not growing rotten fruit anymore.

He saved me. I've got my second chance. I can grow new fruit! I have all the proof I need! Bring on the rewards! I now have the faith I need! It took me six months of looking. Then all of a sudden, I knew that I knew that I knew! Praise God, I am saved! I almost wept with the knowledge of this.

HELPING OTHERS?

*I*t is clear to me now that sin leads to death. I don't want death, I want the new life in Jesus Christ. I want new fruit. I will do whatever I can to make the right choices. By this time, I had done many different studies on subjects in the Bible—things I wanted answers to, and some I felt were necessary but didn't quite know why. I studied topics like the Holy Spirit, church, women, legalism, and money.

Then I felt the need to do a study on anger. I had no idea why this was important to me. I had never really been an angry person. In spite of everything in my life, I was usually upbeat and optimistic. This anger study confused me, but I did it anyway. I read all of the scriptures and copied them down. I put my notes in my binder like all the rest. Then I moved on to the next subject. It just so happened that every time I would get about three fourths of the way through a subject, God would be right there and give me an idea for the next one. I spent most of the month of July doing just this.

Now, Karl and I have always dated. We go out to dinner regularly by ourselves. No matter what the week brings, we always find time to go out. Even though we have been together for ten years, we are still the best of friends and we enjoy each other's company.

We decided to go out one Friday, and as soon as we got in the car, I could tell something was wrong. I didn't know what it was, so I assumed it was me. I must have done something. I asked him what was wrong. He said "nothing." We both got quiet. While we were driving to the restaurant, Karl was snapping at the mistakes of other drivers. He seemed impatient and he hadn't been like that in a while. Since he had been saved, there were many noticeable differences.

This was the "old" Karl coming back to life while I am preparing to have a nice evening with him. We got about half way to the restaurant and he apologized. I had noticed him praying. This was a new thing for me because we don't pray together. I was thrilled to watch his mood completely change after he had prayed.

I then felt comfortable enough to tell him that I had recently done an anger study. He looked at me like he was seeing a ghost. He said, "I can't believe you just used that word!" I said, "Why?" He said, "Because I was just sitting here praying about being angry. I don't know what my problem is, but I have been angry for a week!" I felt my heart lurch. I don't know anything about using the Bible to help someone else with a problem.

I searched my mind to try to remember every message I had read about anger. I was so frustrated. Here I had a chance to actually help someone with something I've learned and I'm drawing a blank. Well, at least now I know why I did the anger study. That was something. I told Karl he could have my notes when we got home and he could see if they helped.

We went into the restaurant and just started talking. The more he talked about what had been going on the last week, the more scriptures kept jumping into my head. Do you remember the 3D picture? I was working too hard, I wanted to be perfect, that's why it wasn't working. As we talked casually, I couldn't remember chapter and verse but I could remember the content of the scriptures that applied.

1 Samuel 11:6 (NLT)
Then the Spirit of God came mightily upon Saul, and he became very angry.

11:6 Anger is a powerful emotion. Often it may drive people to hurt others with words or physical violence. But anger directed at sin and the mistreatment of others is not wrong. Saul was angered by the Ammonites' threat to humiliate and mistreat his fellow Israelites. The Holy Spirit used Saul's anger to bring justice and freedom. When injustice or sin makes you angry, ask God how you can channel that anger in constructive ways to help bring about a positive change.

Mark 3:5 (NLT)
He looked around at them angrily, because he was deeply disturbed by their hard hearts. Then he said to the man, "Reach out your hand." The man reached out his hand, and it became normal again!

3:5 Jesus was angry about the Pharisees' uncaring attitudes. Anger itself is not wrong. It depends on what makes us angry and what we do with our anger. Too often we express our anger in selfish and harmful ways. By contrast, Jesus expressed his anger by correcting a problem—healing the man's hand. Use your anger to find constructive solutions rather than to tear people down.

Ephes. 4:26-27 (NLT)
And "don't sin by letting anger gain control over you." Don't let the sun go down while you are still angry, 27for anger gives a mighty foothold to the Devil.

4:26-27 The Bible doesn't tell us that we shouldn't feel angry, but it points out that it is important to handle our anger properly. If vented thoughtlessly, anger can hurt others and destroy relationships. If bottled up inside, it can cause us to become bitter and destroy us from within. Paul tells us to deal with our anger immediately in a way that builds relationships rather than destroys them. If we nurse our anger, we will give Satan an opportunity to divide us. Are you angry with someone right now? What can you do

to resolve your differences? Don't let the day end before
you begin to work on mending your relationship.

Psalm 30:5 (NLT)
His anger lasts for a moment,
but his favor lasts a lifetime!
Weeping may go on all night,
but joy comes with the morning.

30:5 *Like a shot given by a doctor, the discomfort of*
God's anger lasts only a moment, but the good effects go
on for a long time. Let God's anger be a sharp pain that
warns you to turn from sin.

Psalm 37:8-9 (NLT)
Stop your anger!
Turn from your rage!
Do not envy others—
it only leads to harm.
9For the wicked will be destroyed,
but those who trust in the LORD will possess the land.

37:8-9 *Anger and worry (fretting) are two very destruc-*
tive emotions. They reveal a lack of faith that God loves us
and is in control. We should not worry; instead, we should
trust in God, giving ourselves to him for his use and safe-
keeping. When you dwell on your problems, you will become
anxious and angry. But if you concentrate on God and his
goodness, you will find peace. Where do you focus your at-
tention?

James 1:19-20 (NLT)
My dear brothers and sisters, be quick to listen, slow to
speak, and slow to get angry. 20Your anger can never make
things right in God's sight.

1:19 When we talk too much and listen too little, we communicate to others that we think our ideas are much more important than theirs. James wisely advises us to reverse this process. Put a mental stopwatch on your conversations and keep track of how much you talk and how much you listen. When people talk with you, do they feel that their viewpoints and ideas have value?

1:19-20 These verses speak of anger that erupts when our egos are bruised—"I am hurt;" "My opinions are not being heard." When injustice and sin occur, we should become angry because others are being hurt. But we should not become angry when we fail to win an argument or when we feel offended or neglected. Selfish anger never helps anybody.

Romans 1:18 (NLT)
But God shows his anger from heaven against all sinful, wicked people who push the truth away from themselves.

1:18 Why is God angry at sinful people? Because they have substituted the truth about him with a fantasy of their own imagination (Romans 1:25). They have stifled the truth God naturally reveals to all people in order to believe anything that supports their own self-centered life-styles. God cannot tolerate sin because his nature is morally perfect. He cannot ignore or condone such willful rebellion. God wants to remove the sin and restore the sinner—and he is able to, as long as the sinner does not stubbornly distort or reject the truth. But his anger erupts against those who persist in sinning. Make sure you are not pursuing a fantasy rather than the true God. Don't suppress the truth about him merely to protect your own life-style.

1:18-20 Does anyone have an excuse for not believing

*in God? The Bible answers an emphatic no. God has re-
vealed what he is like in and through his creation. Every
person, therefore, either accepts or rejects God. Don't be
fooled. When the day comes for God to judge your response
to him, no excuses will be accepted. Begin today to give
your devotion and worship to him.*

*1:18-20 In these verses, Paul answers a common objec-
tion: How could a loving God send anyone to hell, especially
someone who has never heard about Christ? In fact, says
Paul, God has revealed himself plainly in the creation to all
people. And yet people reject even this basic knowledge of
God. Also, everyone has an inner sense of what God requires, but they choose not to live up to it. Put another way,
people's moral standards are always better than their behavior. If people suppress God's truth in order to live their
own way, they have no excuse. They know the truth, and
they will have to endure the consequences of ignoring it.*

*1:18-20 Some people wonder why we need missionaries
if people can know about God through nature (the creation).
The answer: (1) Although people know that God exists, they
suppress that truth by their wickedness and thus refuse a
relationship with him. Missionaries sensitively expose their
error and point them to a new beginning. (2) Although people
may believe there is a God, they refuse to commit themselves to him. Missionaries help persuade them, both
through loving words and caring actions. (3) Missionaries
convince people who reject God of the dangerous consequences of their actions. (4) Missionaries help the church
obey the Great Commission of our Lord (Matthew 28:19-
20). (5) Most important, though nature reveals God, people
need to be told about Jesus and how, through him, they can
have a personal relationship with God.*

Knowing that God exists is not enough. People must

learn that God is loving. They must understand what he did to demonstrate his love for us (Romans 5:8). They must be shown how to accept God's forgiveness of their sins. (See also Romans 10:14-15.)

1:20 *What kind of God does nature reveal? Nature shows us a God of might, intelligence, and intricate detail; a God of order and beauty; a God who controls powerful forces. That is general revelation. Through special revelation (the Bible and the coming of Jesus), we learn about God's love and forgiveness, and the promise of eternal life. God has graciously given us both sources that we might fully believe in him.*

1:20 *God reveals his divine nature and personal qualities through creation, even though creation's testimony has been distorted by the fall. Adam's sin resulted in a divine curse upon the whole natural order (Genesis 3:17-19); thorns and thistles were an immediate result, and natural disasters have been common from Adam's day to ours. In Romans 8:19-21, Paul says that nature itself is eagerly awaiting its own redemption from the effects of sin (see Rev. 22:3).*

James 3:6 (NLT)

And the tongue is a flame of fire. It is full of wickedness that can ruin your whole life. It can turn the entire course of your life into a blazing flame of destruction, for it is set on fire by hell itself.

3:6 *James compares the damage the tongue can do to a raging fire—the tongue's wickedness has its source in hell itself. The uncontrolled tongue can do terrible damage. Satan uses the tongue to divide people and pit them against one another. Idle and hateful words are damaging because they spread destruction quickly, and no one can stop the* *results once they are spoken. We dare not be careless with what we say, thinking we can apologize later, because even if we do, the scars remain. A few words spoken in anger can destroy a relationship that took years to build. Before you speak, remember that words are like fire—you can neither control nor reverse the damage they can do.*

I couldn't wait to get home and show him that I remembered. I was able to help someone else. Karl was receptive to the teaching but he did comment on the fact that there were so many rules to follow. I was so happy that God had used me, but I was a little too proud of all the work I had done. I know this is true because something happened a month later that just about crushed me.

I had been taking notes on the Bible for about six weeks. I had been studying day and night. Any opportunity I had was spent reading the Bible doing my topical studies. I was learning so much, so fast, and I loved it. I had wanted knowledge, understanding and wisdom. I was on my way! Karl wasn't spending half as much time in the Bible, and I soon found out that my sister wasn't either.

I called my sister as always and finally noticed that every time I talked to her, I could detect something not quite right. We talked about the Bible mostly. What did you learn lately? What did I learn lately? The normal stuff. There was, however, some underlying doubt in her. It was probably always there but I couldn't hear it before. Now that I knew that I knew that I knew that I was saved, I could sense doubt in her.

I always told my sister everything new that I had learned. I had been especially excited after my salvation study. I told her everything. I told her I hadn't been sure, but now I was. I went over every scripture that jumped out at me and what it meant to me. My sister, who is always excited to see me grow in the Lord, was less than thrilled when I talked about salvation.

What was wrong? I had finally caught up to her, why wasn't

she thrilled? Now we were equal partners in the Lord and we should have had more to talk about. Then my sister pulled the floor out from under my feet. She told me that she wasn't sure that she was saved. She never really had been sure.

I was stunned! I didn't know what to say. How was this possible? Did I miss something? We had been talking for months about this. How could she not know if she was saved? I thought she knew she was saved. Then it dawned on me, I thought. I assumed! Let me let you in on a little secret, God doesn't like it when we assume. If we are assuming something about someone, we are sitting in judgment of that person.

All that time, I assumed she was way ahead of me, and she had actually been growing with me. I had only been behind because I assumed I was behind. My own mind had me convinced that I was less than. God didn't want me to think that way, the enemy did. He had used me and my sister to make the other feel inferior. He had used our Bible study to accomplish this. Since we never discussed who was ahead and who was behind, we were both in our own minds lacking.

It didn't really matter what the enemy had planned, because I had studied this. I had gotten to the other side and I now knew all about salvation. I could help my sister take those final steps. I started with my notes; we talked for several hours each day. We talked for several days each week. I used the Bible. I used Joyce Meyer's teachings. I had been watching Joel Osteen by this time and I used his teachings. I used everything in my arsenal. This went on for two weeks. Nothing had changed.

What was I doing wrong? Why didn't I seem to be getting through? I drove myself crazy. Then at the end of the two weeks God did exactly what he said in 1 Corinthians 1:28-31. *"God chose things despised by the world, things counted as nothing at all, and used them to bring to nothing what the world considers important, [29]so that no one can ever boast in the presence of God. [30]God alone made it possible for you to be in Christ Jesus. For our benefit God made Christ to be wis-*

dom itself. He is the one who made us acceptable to God. He made us pure and holy, and he gave himself to purchase our freedom. [31]As the Scriptures say, "The person who wishes to boast should boast only of what the Lord has done."

Karl and I were on our way to dinner like normal. I was so immersed in my problem with my sister that I couldn't keep it out of our conversation. I didn't want to gossip, but I needed some help. I told Karl what had been going on for the past two weeks. I told him just about everything. I explained that I wasn't sure what I was doing wrong?

He said simply, "Did she ask God if she was saved?" Now it was my turn to look at him like he was a ghost. He smiled. I know that feeling of knowing your helping someone, so I understood the smile. As the scripture was floating around in my head, I told Karl that he had to be the one to call her. It wasn't for me to do. We got to the restaurant and I called my sister. I told her that I was sorry for telling Karl but that she ought to talk to him.

She agreed and he talked to her for about ten minutes. He told her what had happened to him when he had gotten saved. She said she would give it a try and they hung up. Three days later, she called me and said without a doubt that she knew that she knew that she knew.

I knew then that no amount of study could have helped her. She could have read the Bible until she was sick of it and it wouldn't have mattered. God had to put it on her heart. Karl seemed to know that and I couldn't figure it out. For all my studying, I didn't have the answer. God used the things counted as nothing and used them to bring to nothing what the world considers important. What was important to me? Studying, knowing, understanding. He used it against me to show me that without God none of it matters. He won't use me if I want to be used so that I can say, "Look what I did!"

I was immediately and irreversibly humbled. I understood at

that moment that it wasn't about me. I have a relationship with God, but so does everyone else. Don't make the mistake of thinking that you are going to do better than God at his own relationship with someone else. Everyone has their own relationship and everyone has the same rights that you do. You can explain what God has done in your life, because it may help someone else.

But one thing I learned about God is that I cannot dictate how someone else's relationship is going to work. Just because God used something and it worked for me, doesn't mean it will work for everyone. He deals with everyone in their own way. Would I have let someone tell me how my relationship with God should be going? Let's think about it. *NO*!!!

Why then would God want me to interfere with someone else's relationship with him? God gave me a permanent attitude change. Another free gift, I can't even count them anymore. I can't accept credit for anything! I am happy when I can say, "Don't thank me, thank God." I am happy when I can say, "It wasn't me, it was God." I am happy when I can say, "God showed me this way, you should ask Him to show you."

That started a new walk with God. He was on my mind all the time now. There is so much to learn and yet so much that I have learned already. As I started August, something was nagging at me.

Have you ever heard of the Ten Commandments?

*O*nce I knew that I was saved, I wanted to avoid the pitfalls. I didn't know how to do that but I was going to find out. I didn't want to make the same old dumb mistakes that I had made in the past. I needed to know what I could do and what I shouldn't be doing. Karl had mentioned all of the rules we needed to follow and it was nagging at me.

Exodus 20:1-17 (NLT)
Then God instructed the people as follows:
²"I am the LORD your God, who rescued you from slavery in Egypt.
³"Do not worship any other gods besides me.
⁴"Do not make idols of any kind, whether in the shape of birds or animals or fish. ⁵You must never worship or bow down to them, for I, the LORD your God, am a jealous God who will not share your affection with any other god! I do not leave unpunished the sins of those who hate me, but I punish the children for the sins of their parents to the third and fourth generations. ⁶But I lavish my love on those who love me and obey my commands, even for a thousand generations.
⁷"Do not misuse the name of the LORD your God. The LORD will not let you go unpunished if you misuse his name.
⁸"Remember to observe the Sabbath day by keeping it holy. ⁹Six days a week are set apart for your daily duties and regular work, ¹⁰but the seventh day is a day of rest

dedicated to the LORD your God. On that day no one in your household may do any kind of work. This includes you, your sons and daughters, your male and female servants, your livestock, and any foreigners living among you. ¹¹For in six days the LORD made the heavens, the earth, the sea, and everything in them; then he rested on the seventh day. That is why the LORD blessed the Sabbath day and set it apart as holy.

¹²"Honor your father and mother. Then you will live a long, full life in the land the LORD your God will give you.

¹³"Do not murder.

¹⁴"Do not commit adultery.

¹⁵"Do not steal.

¹⁶"Do not testify falsely against your neighbor.

¹⁷"Do not covet your neighbor's house. Do not covet your neighbor's wife, male or female servant, ox or donkey, or anything else your neighbor owns."

I was directed to these laws one day in August. I circled around them and I didn't know what I was supposed to see. I read them and re-read them. I knew that I needed something from them but I couldn't see it and I decided to leave it alone for a while. I am pretty sure I had just been studying legalism before this Ten-Commandments problem I was having.

In my legalism study, I was learning about following the rules. I had heard many comments about there being so many rules in the Bible and no one will ever be able to follow them all. I know that I am not perfect and I can't memorize all the things God wants me to remember. I am sure I will mess up somewhere. How will I know when to ask for forgiveness? How could I avoid or at least reduce the number of times that I make these mistakes?

I remembered a verse from my love study. In John 14:21 it says, *"Those who obey my commandments are the ones who love me. And because they love me, my Father will love them, and I will love them. And I will reveal myself to each one of them."* I wanted to do this to the best of my ability.

I knew God didn't want us to just follow a set of rules like robots, but I had to do the legalism study to find out what he did want us to do. I learned that Matthew 5:17 says, *"Don't misunderstand why I have come. I did not come to abolish the law of Moses or the writings of the prophets. No, I came to fulfill them."*

Then I read Matthew 5:21-22 where it says, *"You have heard that the law of Moses says, 'Do not murder. If you commit murder, you are subject to judgment.' ²²But I say, if you are angry with someone, you are subject to judgment! If you call someone an idiot, you are in danger of being brought before the high council. And if you curse someone, you are in danger of the fires of hell."* Apparently, I am in big trouble.

Next, I read Matthew 12:10-12 and it says, *"where he noticed a man with a deformed hand. The Pharisees asked Jesus, "Is it legal to work by healing on the Sabbath day?" (They were, of course, hoping he would say yes, so they could bring charges against him.) ¹¹And he answered, "If you had one sheep, and it fell into a well on the Sabbath, wouldn't you get to work and pull it out? Of course you would. ¹²And how much more valuable is a person than a sheep! Yes, it is right to do good on the Sabbath."* So, I am thoroughly confused. Do we follow the commandments or don't we?

I knew God knew I was not seeing the big picture. I just wasn't getting this. All I could see in this area was contradiction, and worse, that was all I was focusing on. I read the Ten Commandments again and I knew there was something there, but I was focused on the words on the page. I was not focusing on the meaning.

I left it alone for a day. I tried again but this time I could feel there was something on the verge of showing itself. The something was taking its time and I had other things to do. I had been so caught up in my studies that this was an interruption. I am not learning anything by being stuck on this. I left it alone again. This went on for about a week.

I finally asked out loud, "what is it with the Ten Commandments? I don't get it, Lord. What am I supposed to see?" He said, "Read them—who are they for?" What do you mean who are they for? They are for me. I am supposed to follow the laws. Then he said, "Why?"

I started to say, "because you said so," and then something stopped me. There is a reason! What is the reason for the Ten Commandments? What would be the purpose? Who do they benefit? Just then it hit me! Every single one benefits someone other than me.

If I were the only person on earth, none of these laws would be necessary. Look at them again and see why you get into trouble for breaking the laws. I don't mean read them and see the obvious problems with breaking these kinds of laws. I mean look just below the surface and see them from God's point of view.

I have been a mom for sixteen years. All moms know the pivotal point in a child's life is kindergarten. Not just because they are starting school, but, "they are no longer yours once they go to school." I would be surprised if every mom hasn't either heard this or said this at some point in their lives. Why would they no longer be yours? Because they will be influenced by other children to do things that you didn't teach them. They will be influenced by other children to say things that you didn't teach them. They will be influenced by other children to act differently than you taught them.

Keeping in mind that we are created in God's image, why would He be any different? He gave us the Ten Commandments so that we would not negatively affect his other children. Think about it—every commandment represents you doing something in front of other people, with other people, or to other people. No matter how you look at it, it is because of other people that he gave us these laws.

He doesn't want us to negatively affect any of his children. He does want us to positively affect all of his children.

Remember, God loves all, God wants all. Not just me, but you and everyone else. This is why in the New Testament it says in Mark 12:29-31, *"One of the teachers of religious law was standing there listening to the discussion. He realized that Jesus had answered well, so he asked, "Of all the commandments, which is the most important?" [29]Jesus replied, "The most important commandment is this: 'Hear, O Israel! The Lord our God is the one and only Lord. [30]And you must love the Lord your God with all your heart, all your soul, all your mind, and all your strength.' [31]The second is equally important: 'Love your neighbor as yourself.' No other commandment is greater than these."*

In John 13:34 it says, *"So now I am giving you a new commandment: Love each other. Just as I have loved you, you should love each other."*

And, finally, in Romans 13:9-10 it says, *"For the commandments against adultery and murder and stealing and coveting—and any other commandment—are all summed up in this one commandment: "Love your neighbor as yourself." [10]Love does no wrong to anyone, so love satisfies all of God's requirements."*

God was changing my heart attitude. He was making me see that I would know when I sinned because anything not done in love is a sin. I would know in my heart when I was making a mistake. Then I could stop it or at least apologize for it afterward. I would on the reverse side be able to take my time and make sure that anything I was doing was being done out of love to avoid the mistakes. Either way, I would know.

I managed to find a scripture in my Holy Spirit study that shows this with crystal clarity. In Galatians 5:19-25 it says, *"When you follow the desires of your sinful nature, your lives will produce these evil results: sexual immorality, impure thoughts, eagerness for lustful pleasure, [20]idolatry, participation in demonic activities, hostility, quarreling, jealousy, outbursts of anger, selfish ambition, divisions, the feeling that everyone is wrong except those in your own little group, 21envy, drunkenness, wild parties, and other kinds of sin. Let me tell you again, as I have before, that anyone living that sort of life will not inherit the Kingdom of God.*

22But when the Holy Spirit controls our lives, he will produce this kind of fruit in us: love, joy, peace, patience, kindness, goodness, faithfulness, 23gentleness, and self-control. Here there is no conflict with the law.

24Those who belong to Christ Jesus have nailed the passions and desires of their sinful nature to his cross and crucified them there. 25If we are living now by the Holy Spirit, let us follow the Holy Spirit's leading in every part of our lives.

I suddenly realized that the Ten Commandments didn't just apply to me, they apply to everyone. I can only control my actions, not everyone else's. I am only going to be accountable for my actions, not everyone else's. No excuse will be acceptable. I have no one to blame. I now know how I have to act. I have to recognize that if I am not acting with love, joy, peace, patience, kindness, goodness, faithfulness, gentleness, and self control, I need to back up and reevaluate. There is going to be some reason that I need forgiveness.

And, if this is true for me, it is true for everyone. I am starting to notice how other people act. I am starting to recognize other Christians. I am also starting to recognize all the people who obviously don't know all that I have learned. Who is going to tell them? How do I make them understand that this is a life and death decision they have to make? And either decision is eternal. All of a sudden I am wishing that I knew what to do. Now, I am worried!

HOW DO YOU FEEL ABOUT MONEY?

Now, you can get ready for some name dropping. In late August, I found Trinity Broadcasting Network on my television. I felt like I found a treasure chest. All Christian television all day. I was introduced to T D Jakes, Creflo Dollar, Jesse Duplantis, Benny Hinn, Kenneth & Gloria Copeland, John Hagee and many more. I had been watching Joyce Meyer, Joel Osteen, *The 700 Club*, and James & Betty Robinson on another channel.

The reason I name them is because, to me, they are my big brothers and sisters in Jesus. They all have at one time or another touched my heart with a message that gave me direction for my studies. Two of the studies were tithing and worry. As a matter of fact, one caused the other for a time.

I don't want to give anyone the impression that during all this time, I was not worrying. I was worrying about everything. I was still worried about our debt. I was worried about not being in the will of God by living with Karl instead of marrying him. I was worried about my kids' relationships with Jesus. I was worried about anyone that didn't know Jesus. God knew I was worried about everything even though I regularly gave everything up to him to handle. I didn't complain out loud anymore and I acted like I wasn't worried, but God knew in my heart I was very worried.

I was also, however, consumed with worry over our financial situation. It was always there, ready to take over my thoughts. In Proverbs 18:11 it says, *"The rich think of their wealth as an impregnable defense; they imagine it is a high wall of safety."* I can guarantee you that when we were "rich" I didn't worry much. We weren't going to have any real problems. We could afford to face any problem that we could imagine. Of course, we hadn't been thinking of problems that we couldn't imagine.

Now, I had been praying for a miracle to at least get us even so we could start again. Shortly after Karl got saved, God started opening doors for us. All of a sudden, customers that hadn't talked to us in months, remembered we existed. All of a sudden, jobs were plentiful. All of a sudden, Karl was working 50 hours a week. Our business was being restored, slowly, but it was being restored.

I was watching *The 700 Club* one night, and the message was about tithing. I thought there was no way. I was tithing at my church and I couldn't afford any more. Then God put it on my heart to become a partner. I called and said I could only give $50 per month. The woman on the other end of the phone was thrilled. I had been thinking that $50 wasn't a drop in the bucket to these people. Here the woman acted like I had given her the money.

I have to admit it felt great. I really felt like I had done something good. I had listened to the message about giving to the kingdom and it being returned to you 100 fold. This will sound shallow, but I thought, "My bank can't give me that kind of return!" Sign me up. I had only been giving to my church, and now that my tithing had increased, my blessings should increase. When you have financial problems you just can't seem to get them off your mind.

Afterwards, I realized that my small amount had been added to thousands of other small amounts and that does mean something to the kingdom. Now I felt like I really contributed something to God. Shortly after this, I became a partner with Joyce Meyer ministries and Life Outreach Ministries.

I stepped up the praying for my miracle. I know that God is going to get me my miracle. I don't know how, but I know he will get me my miracle. He does not want me in this condition and only he can change my circumstances. He does have to be fair, but he is also the miracle maker. This is all I have to hold onto while I am struggling. I know there is no earthly way for me to earn the kind of money I need to get right with him, out of debt and able to contribute without worry.

One day at the end of August, I am ashamed to say that I was looking for something in Karl's truck and I found some money. More money than I thought we even had. I was immediately attacked by the enemy. What can he possibly be doing with all this cash? Is he really working during the day? Is he doing something on the side and not telling me about it? I am not perfect. The "old" Liz comes back with a vengeance occasionally.

I figured if he could hold onto that much money, so could I. The next big payment we received, I cashed a check for $1,000 (in $100 bills) and put it in a drawer. If he finds out, I was already prepared to confront him about the money he had. I never had that much cash sitting around. I was guilty from the time I wrote the check, but that didn't stop me. And I didn't tell Karl.

Now this money is sitting in this drawer driving me crazy. I felt so guilty. I had been doing so well, and now this. What do I do with the money? I know what I can do with the money, there are always homeless people around. I can't just give them the money, however. How will they know that it is from God? I could make up four-by-six-inch cards with some scriptures on them, then they would know. At least I would be doing something in the name of the Lord.

I got to the office supply store with a whole plan. Then I noticed this preprinted letterhead with footprints and a cross. I thought, "I can fit more scriptures on there!" I bought the letterhead and went home. I already had some scriptures in mind about love and salvation. Now, I am on a mission! When I got home, I worked on the letters until they were just the way I wanted them.

I made a decision to cash a $100 bill and make $10 bills out of it, then I would put $10 in each envelope. I would keep them in my car and every time I saw one of those homeless people, I would give them one. I did that and then I drove around for a month and never saw one homeless person. In the meantime, anytime I needed money I would go out to my car and borrow $10. Before I knew it, the envelopes were empty.

I decided to try again. On September 29th, I put a $100 bill in my wallet. I figured I would go to the bank the next day and cash it in for the $10 bills. I woke up on September 30th and took my daughter to school as always. It was raining that morning and I could barely see to drive. I was thinking, "What a good day to go to a diner and get breakfast and read the paper." I didn't have any reason to go right home, so I took myself to breakfast.

Breakfast was excellent and the waitress brought the bill. It cost about $9. I opened my purse to get the money and immediately I heard, "Leave the $100 bill as a tip." Oh, you have got to be kidding! I don't think so! Get behind me Satan (I convinced myself that he was trying to steal God's money). I did, however, leave everything else I had in my wallet (about $17).

I got in my car and had a funny feeling. I ignored it as best I could. I got home and turned on Joyce Meyer like always. She was saying, "If you want your prayers answered, you need to be obedient." I turned the television off and got back in my car. I drove back to the restaurant and put the $100 in one of my envelopes.

I walked in and told the waitress, "This is the tip I wanted to leave earlier, and if I didn't come back, I wouldn't have been able to live with myself for the rest of the day!" I got in my car and I was shaking from head to toe. I can guarantee you there is no feeling you can get artificially that compares to knowing you were obedient. I was flying high the rest of the day. I have never had a rush like that.

What the enemy plans for evil, God will make good. This seemed to run around my mind all day. The following night,

Karl and I went to dinner and I told him everything. I couldn't help myself. I told him about finding the money and doubting him. I couldn't seem to apologize enough. He tried to explain that he needs cash for supplies because we are on a COD basis with all of our suppliers and I knew this was true and felt worse. I apologized over and over. I asked him if I could still use the money for random acts of kindness and he said, "Of course!"

God showed me my relationship with money and I was terribly ashamed. It was obvious that although I thought I trusted God with everything, I didn't seem to trust him with the money issue or this little thing with Karl. He showed me that if I was worrying, I was not trusting him. I didn't want to worry. I went home and looked up the word worry in the back of my Bible.

WORRY FOR NOTHING

*T*his incident with the money had a twofold effect. I saw all of my worries and I saw where I seemed to be the most vulnerable. These are some of the scriptures that were referenced:

Proverbs 20:24 (NLT)
How can we understand the road we travel? It is the LORD *who directs our steps.*

20:24 *We are often confused by the events around us. Many things we will never understand; others will fall into place in years to come as we look back and see how God was working. This proverb counsels us not to worry if we don't understand everything as it happens. Instead, we should trust that God knows what he's doing, even if his timing or design is not clear to us. See Psalm 37:23 for a reassuring promise of God's direction in your life.*

Matthew 6:25 (NLT)
"So I tell you, don't worry about everyday life—whether you have enough food, drink, and clothes. Doesn't life consist of more than food and clothing?

6:25 *Because of the ill effects of worry, Jesus tells us not to worry about those needs that God promises to supply. Worry may (1) damage your health, (2) cause the object of your worry to consume your thoughts, (3) disrupt your productivity, (4) negatively affect the way you treat others, and*

My First Year in the Lord's Family

(5) reduce your ability to trust in God. How many ill effects of worry are you experiencing? Here is the difference between worry and genuine concern—worry immobilizes, but concern moves you to action.

Matthew 6:34 (NLT)
"So don't worry about tomorrow, for tomorrow will bring its own worries. Today's trouble is enough for today.

6:34 *Planning for tomorrow is time well spent; worrying about tomorrow is time wasted. Sometimes it's difficult to tell the difference. Careful planning is thinking ahead about goals, steps, and schedules, and trusting in God's guidance. When done well, planning can help alleviate worry. Worriers, by contrast, are consumed by fear and find it difficult to trust God. They let their plans interfere with their relationship with God. Don't let worries about tomorrow affect your relationship with God today.*

Matthew 10:19-20 (NLT)
When you are arrested, don't worry about what to say in your defense, because you will be given the right words at the right time. ²⁰For it won't be you doing the talking—it will be the Spirit of your Father speaking through you.

10:19-20 *Jesus told the disciples that when arrested for preaching the gospel, they should not worry about what to say in their defense—God's Spirit would speak through them. This promise was fulfilled in Acts 4:8-14 and elsewhere. Some mistakenly think this means we don't have to prepare to present the gospel because God will take care of everything. Scripture teaches, however, that we are to make carefully prepared, thoughtful statements (Col. 4:6). Jesus is not telling us to stop preparing but to stop worrying.*

Liz Kraus

Luke 12:22-34 (NLT)

Then turning to his disciples, Jesus said, "So I tell you, don't worry about everyday life—whether you have enough food to eat or clothes to wear. ²³For life consists of far more than food and clothing. ²⁴Look at the ravens. They don't need to plant or harvest or put food in barns because God feeds them. And you are far more valuable to him than any birds! ²⁵Can all your worries add a single moment to your life? Of course not! ²⁶And if worry can't do little things like that, what's the use of worrying over bigger things?

²⁷"Look at the lilies and how they grow. They don't work or make their clothing, yet Solomon in all his glory was not dressed as beautifully as they are. ²⁸And if God cares so wonderfully for flowers that are here today and gone tomorrow, won't he more surely care for you? You have so little faith! ²⁹And don't worry about food—what to eat and drink. Don't worry whether God will provide it for you. ³⁰These things dominate the thoughts of most people, but your Father already knows your needs. ³¹He will give you all you need from day to day if you make the Kingdom of God your primary concern.

³²"So don't be afraid, little flock. For it gives your Father great happiness to give you the Kingdom.

³³"Sell what you have and give to those in need. This will store up treasure for you in heaven! And the purses of heaven have no holes in them. Your treasure will be safe— no thief can steal it and no moth can destroy it. ³⁴Wherever your treasure is, there your heart and thoughts will also be.

12:22-34 *Jesus commands us not to worry. But how can we avoid it? Only faith can free us from the anxiety caused by greed and covetousness. It is good to work and plan responsibly; it is bad to dwell on all the ways our planning could go wrong. Worry is pointless because it can't fill any of our needs; worry is foolish because the Creator of the*

90

universe loves us and knows what we need. He promises to meet all our real needs, but not necessarily all our desires.

12:31 *Seeking the kingdom of God means making Jesus the Lord and King of your life. He must control every area— your work, play, plans, relationships. Is the kingdom only one of your many concerns, or is it central to all you do? Are you holding back any areas of your life from God's control? As Lord and Creator, he wants to help provide what you need as well as guide how you use what he provides.*

12:33 *Money seen as an end in itself quickly traps us and cuts us off from both God and the needy. The key to using money wisely is to see how much we can use for God's purposes, not how much we can accumulate for ourselves. Does God's love touch your wallet? Does your money free you to help others? If so, you are storing up lasting treasures in heaven. If your financial goals and possessions hinder you from giving generously, loving others, or serving God, sell what you must to bring your life into perspective.*

12:34 *If you concentrate your money in your business, your thoughts will center on making the business profitable. If you direct it toward other people, you will become concerned with their welfare. Where do you put your time, money, and energy? What do you think about most? How should you change the way you use your resources in order to reflect kingdom values more accurately?*

Philip. 4:6-7 (NLT)
Don't worry about anything; instead, pray about everything. Tell God what you need, and thank him for all he has done. ⁷If you do this, you will experience God's peace, which is far more wonderful than the human mind can understand.

His peace will guard your hearts and minds as you live in Christ Jesus.

4:6-7 Imagine never being "anxious about anything"! It seems like an impossibility—we all have worries on the job, in our homes, at school. But Paul's advice is to turn our worries into prayers. Do you want to worry less? Then pray more! Whenever you start to worry, stop and pray.

4:7 God's peace is different from the world's peace (see John 14:27). True peace is not found in positive thinking, in absence of conflict, or in good feelings. It comes from knowing that God is in control. Our citizenship in Christ's kingdom is sure, our destiny is set, and we can have victory over sin. Let God's peace guard your heart against anxiety.

I was surprised to find that every scripture seemed to be saying basically the same thing. I flipped back to my salvation study (the one I was sure I understood) and I realized that although I am saved, I have not trusted God in almost any area of my life. I was proving by my worry that I didn't believe!

I had been worried about everything. I loved it when God pulled me through time and again. But at no time did I actually trust him to pull me through. How could I get so far and then realize I never even took the first step? I mean, I had been learning and taking it to my heart. The evidence of this was showing itself all over my life. All the changes had been for the good. I had relapses, but the funny thing was that my family was more shocked when the "old" Liz came back than they had been when the "new" Liz started to emerge. I seemed to be kinder and more merciful. I seemed to have an abundance of patience. Everyone noticed, and they changed as well. Karl even noticed that our moods affected the mood of the entire house.

We were really trying our best and it seemed to be working.

The only "bad" days seemed to be when we were worrying about something. I'll bet we had at least four incidents a week. Someone was worried about something and said something to someone else and this either caused more worry or an argument.

Who do we sound like? If you don't know, read the Old Testament some time, particularly Exodus. We are acting like the Israelites. They were free from Egypt and what did they do? They complained about their worries! I wish I could quote the person who said this, but I once heard someone talking about the Israelites. He or she said, "God didn't punish them for complaining, God punished them for complaining to each other."

Do you remember what God showed me about the Ten Commandments? Do not negatively influence any of his children. I learned it but I didn't recognize worry as a problem. I do now! I am actually showing a lack of faith when I worry.

I think the scripture Philippians 4:6-7 helped me solve this problem the best. I still quote this scripture almost every day. Every single time I feel the worry coming, I stop and quote this scripture to remind myself to have faith. Right after that, I have a "remind God session." I remind God that I am still worried about this problem, I give it to him and tell him I am trusting him to take care of me. I then profusely thank him for everything.

I have thanked him for hot, clean water for a shower. I have thanked him for sending Jesus. I have thanked Jesus for coming and paying the price. And I have thanked him for just about everything in between. I found myself thanking him more than anything else. I still prayed about everything, but I found I spent more time thanking him than anything. What did I really have to worry about? *If God is with me, who can be against me* (Romans 8:31). *No weapon formed against me can prosper* (Isaiah 54:17).

I remember one day Karl called me and told me that he forgot to take the garbage can out to the curb. We have a stone driveway and a large garbage can. The garbage can won't roll on stones easily. I started down the driveway and the complaining began immediately. I got down to the curb and I was devastated. I realized that everything I complained about could be taken away from me. I could see myself living in a shack and throwing the garbage out the window.

I turned around and thanked God for everything I had just complained about. I thanked him for a big front yard and a long driveway. I thanked him for my health, and that I was able to walk down that driveway and was strong enough to pull a large garbage can. I thanked him for every product that produced all the garbage.

I needed to stop worrying and complaining and start praying. I don't want to offend God. I needed to pray for forgiveness. I needed to pray for strength. I needed to pray for His guidance. What should my next study be? How about prayer?

PRAY FOR EVERYTHING

*I*t's funny to me that I started this year praying to God to help me. Now, here I have come full circle and the most important thing is prayer. My prayer study was one of the largest studies next to salvation. I am including various scriptures that I found.

Philip. 4:6-7 (NLT)
Don't worry about anything; instead, pray about everything. Tell God what you need, and thank him for all he has done. ⁷If you do this, you will experience God's peace, which is far more wonderful than the human mind can understand. His peace will guard your hearts and minds as you live in Christ Jesus.

4:6-7 Imagine never being "anxious about anything"! It seems like an impossibility—we all have worries on the job, in our homes, at school. But Paul's advice is to turn our worries into prayers. Do you want to worry less? Then pray more! Whenever you start to worry, stop and pray.

4:7 God's peace is different from the world's peace (see John 14:27). True peace is not found in positive thinking, in absence of conflict, or in good feelings. It comes from knowing that God is in control. Our citizenship in Christ's kingdom is sure, our destiny is set, and we can have victory over sin. Let God's peace guard your heart against anxiety.

Matthew 26:40-41 (NLT)
Then he returned to the disciples and found them asleep. He said to Peter, "Couldn't you stay awake and watch with

*me even one hour? ⁴¹Keep alert and pray. Otherwise temp-
tation will overpower you. For though the spirit is willing
enough, the body is weak!"*

26:40-41 *Jesus used Peter's drowsiness to warn him
about the kinds of temptation he would soon face. The way
to overcome temptation is to keep watch and pray. Watching means being aware of the possibilities of temptation,
sensitive to the subtleties, and spiritually equipped to fight
it. Because temptation strikes where we are most vulnerable,
we can't resist it alone. Prayer is essential because God's
strength can shore up our defenses and defeat Satan's power.*

Exodus 14:15 (NLT)
*Then the LORD said to Moses, "Why are you crying out
to me? Tell the people to get moving!*

14:15 *The Lord told Moses to stop praying and get moving! Prayer must have a vital place in our lives, but there is
also a place for action. Sometimes we know what to do, but
we pray for more guidance as an excuse to postpone doing
it. If we know what we should do, then it is time to get
moving.*

Psalm 3:5 (NLT)
*I lay down and slept.
I woke up in safety,
for the LORD was watching over me.*

3:5 *Sleep does not come easily during a crisis. David
could have had sleepless nights when his son Absalom re-
belled and gathered an army to kill him. But he slept
peacefully, even during the rebellion. What made the difference? David cried out to the Lord, and the Lord heard him.
The assurance of answered prayer brings peace. It is easier*

to sleep well when we have full assurance that God is in control of circumstances. If you are lying awake at night worrying about circumstances you can't change, pour out your heart to God, and thank him that he is in control. Then sleep will come.

Psalm 5:1-3 (NLT)
For the choir director: A psalm of David, to be accompanied by the flute.
O Lord, hear me as I pray;
pay attention to my groaning.
²Listen to my cry for help, my King and my God,
for I will never pray to anyone but you.
³Listen to my voice in the morning, Lord.
Each morning I bring my requests to you and wait expectantly.

5:1-3 The secret of a close relationship with God is to pray to him earnestly each morning. In the morning, our minds are more free from problems and then we can commit the whole day to God. Regular communication helps any friendship and is certainly necessary for a strong relationship with God. We need to communicate with him daily. Do you have a regular time to pray and read God's Word?

Matthew 6:5-8 (NLT)
"And now about prayer. When you pray, don't be like the hypocrites who love to pray publicly on street corners and in the synagogues where everyone can see them. I assure you, that is all the reward they will ever get. ⁶But when you pray, go away by yourself, shut the door behind you, and pray to your Father secretly. Then your Father, who knows all secrets, will reward you.
⁷"When you pray, don't babble on and on as people of other religions do. They think their prayers are answered

only by repeating their words again and again. ⁸Don't be like them, because your Father knows exactly what you need even before you ask him!

6:5-6 *Some people, especially the religious leaders, wanted to be seen as "holy," and public prayer was one way to get attention. Jesus saw through their self-righteous acts, however, and taught that the essence of prayer is not public style but private communication with God. There is a place for public prayer, but to pray only where others will notice you indicates that your real audience is not God.*

Col. 4:2 (NLT)
Devote yourselves to prayer with an alert mind and a thankful heart.

4:2 *Have you ever grown tired of praying for something or someone? Paul says we should "devote" ourselves to prayer and be "watchful" in prayer. Our persistence is an expression of our faith that God answers our prayers. Faith shouldn't die if the answers come slowly, for the delay may be God's way of working his will in our lives. When you feel tired of praying, know that God is present, always listening, always answering—maybe not in ways you had hoped, but in ways that he knows are best.*

Matthew 7:9-11 (NLT)
You parents—if your children ask for a loaf of bread, do you give them a stone instead? ¹⁰Or if they ask for a fish, do you give them a snake? Of course not! ¹¹If you sinful people know how to give good gifts to your children, how much more will your heavenly Father give good gifts to those who ask him.

7:9-10 The child in Jesus' example asked his father for bread and fish—good and necessary items. If the child had asked for a poisonous snake, would the wise father have granted his request? Sometimes God knows we are praying for "snakes" and does not give us what we ask for, even though we persist in our prayers. As we learn to know God better as a loving Father, we learn to ask for what is good for us, and then he grants it.

Mark 11:22-23 (NLT)

Then Jesus said to the disciples, "Have faith in God. [23]I assure you that you can say to this mountain, 'May God lift you up and throw you into the sea,' and your command will be obeyed. All that's required is that you really believe and do not doubt in your heart.

11:22-23 The kind of prayer that moves mountains is prayer for the fruitfulness of God's kingdom. It would seem impossible to move a mountain into the sea, so Jesus used that picture to say that God can do anything. God will answer your prayers, but not as a result of your positive mental attitude. Other conditions must be met: (1) you must be a believer; (2) you must not hold a grudge against another person; (3) you must not pray with selfish motives; (4) your request must be for the good of God's kingdom. To pray effectively, you need faith in God, not faith in the object of your request. If you focus only on your request, you will be left with nothing if your request is refused.

11:24 Jesus, our example for prayer, prayed, "Everything is possible for you . . . Yet not what I will, but what you will" (Mark 14:36). Our prayers are often motivated by our own interests and desires. We like to hear that we can have anything. But Jesus prayed with God's interests in mind. When we pray, we should express our desires, but want his will above ours. Check yourself to see if your prayers focus on your interests or God's.

John 17:20 (NLT)

"I am praying not only for these disciples but also for all who will ever believe in me because of their testimony.

17:20 *Jesus prayed for all who would follow him, including you and others you know. He prayed for unity (John 17:11), protection from the evil one (John 17:15), and sanctity (holiness) (John 17:17). Knowing that Jesus prayed for us should give us confidence as we work for his kingdom.*

Col. 1:9-14 (NLT)

So we have continued praying for you ever since we first heard about you. We ask God to give you a complete understanding of what he wants to do in your lives, and we ask him to make you wise with spiritual wisdom. [10]Then the way you live will always honor and please the Lord, and you will continually do good, kind things for others. All the while, you will learn to know God better and better.

[11]We also pray that you will be strengthened with his glorious power so that you will have all the patience and endurance you need. May you be filled with joy, [12]always thanking the Father, who has enabled you to share the inheritance that belongs to God's holy people, who live in the light. [13]For he has rescued us from the one who rules in the kingdom of darkness, and he has brought us into the Kingdom of his dear Son. [14]God has purchased our freedom with his blood and has forgiven all our sins.

1:9-14 *Paul was exposing a heresy in the Colossian church that was similar to Gnosticism (see the note on +Col. 2:4ff for more information). Gnostics valued the accumulation of knowledge, but Paul pointed out that knowledge* *in itself is empty. To be worth anything, it must lead to a changed life and right living. His prayer for the Colossians has two dimensions: (1) that they might be filled with the knowledge of God's will through all spiritual wisdom and understanding, and (2) that they would bear fruit in every good work, growing in the knowledge of God. Knowledge is not merely to be accumulated; it should give us direction for living. Paul wanted the Colossians to be wise, but he also wanted them to use their knowledge. Knowledge of God is not a secret that only a few can discover; it is open to everyone. God wants us to learn more about him, and also to put belief into practice by helping others.*

1:9-14 Sometimes we wonder how to pray for missionaries and other leaders we have never met. Paul had never met the Colossians, but he faithfully prayed for them. His prayers teach us how to pray for others, whether we know them or not. We can request that they (1) understand God's will, (2) gain spiritual wisdom, (3) please and honor God, (4) bear good fruit, (5) grow in the knowledge of God, (6) be filled with God's strength, (7) have great endurance and patience, (8) stay full of Christ's joy, and (9) give thanks always. All believers have these same basic needs. When you don't know how to pray for someone, use Paul's prayer pattern for the Colossians.

1:12-14 Paul lists five benefits God gives all believers through Christ: (1) he made us qualified to share his inheritance (see also 2 Cor. 5:21); (2) he rescued us from Satan's dominion of darkness and made us his children (see also Col. 2:15); (3) he brought us into his eternal kingdom (see also Ephes. 1:5-6); (4) he redeemed us—bought our freedom from sin and judgment (see also Hebrews 9:12); and (5) he forgave all our sins (see also Ephes. 1:7). Thank God for what you have received in Christ.

1:13 *The Colossians feared the unseen forces of dark-ness, but Paul says that true believers have been transferred from darkness to light, from slavery to freedom, from guilt to forgiveness, and from the power of Satan to the power of God. We have been rescued from a rebel kingdom to serve the rightful King. Our conduct should reflect our new alle-giance.*

1 Tim. 2:1-4 (NLT)
I urge you, first of all, to pray for all people. As you make your requests, plead for God's mercy upon them, and give thanks. ²Pray this way for kings and all others who are in authority, so that we can live in peace and quietness, in godliness and dignity. ³This is good and pleases God our Savior, ⁴for he wants everyone to be saved and to under-stand the truth.

2:1-4 *Although God is all-powerful and all-knowing, he has chosen to let us help him change the world through our prayers. How this works is a mystery to us because of our limited understanding, but it is a reality. Paul urges us to pray for each other and for our leaders in government. Our earnest prayers will have powerful results (James 5:16).*

2:2 *When our lives are going along peacefully and qui-etly, it is difficult to remember to pray for those in authority, because we often take good government for granted. It's easier to remember to pray when we experience problems. But we should pray for those in authority around the world so that their societies will be conducive to the spread of the gospel.*

2:4 *Both Peter and Paul said that God wants all to be saved (see 2 Peter 3:9). This does not mean that all will be saved, because the Bible makes it clear that many reject*

Christ (Matthew 25:31-46; John 12:44-50; Hebrews 10:26-29). The gospel message has a universal scope; it is not directed only to people of one race, one sex, or one national background. God loves the whole world and sent his Son to save sinners. Never assume that anyone is outside God's mercy or beyond the reach of his offer of salvation.

James 4:2-3 (NLT)

You want what you don't have, so you scheme and kill to get it. You are jealous for what others have, and you can't possess it, so you fight and quarrel to take it away from them. And yet the reason you don't have what you want is that you don't ask God for it. ³And even when you do ask, you don't get it because your whole motive is wrong—you want only what will give you pleasure.

4:1-3 Conflicts and disputes among believers are always harmful. James explains that these quarrels result from evil desires battling within us—we want more possessions, more money, higher status, more recognition. When we want badly enough to fulfill these desires, we fight in order to do so. Instead of aggressively grabbing what we want, we should submit ourselves to God, ask God to help us get rid of our selfish desires, and trust him to give us what we really need.

4:2-3 James mentions the most common problems in prayer: not asking, asking for the wrong things, asking for the wrong reasons. Do you talk to God at all? When you do, what do you talk about? Do you ask only to satisfy your desires? Do you seek God's approval for what you already plan to do? Your prayers will become powerful when you allow God to change your desires so that they perfectly correspond to his will for you (1 John 3:21-22).

4:3-4 There is nothing wrong with wanting a pleasurable life. God gives us good gifts that he wants us to enjoy (James 1:17; Ephes. 4:7; 1 Tim. 4:4-5). But having friendship with the world involves seeking pleasure at others' expense or at the expense of obeying God. Pleasure that keeps us from pleasing God is sinful; pleasure from God's rich bounty is good.

4:4-6 The cure for evil desires is humility (see Proverbs 16:18-19; 1 Peter 5:5-6). Pride makes us self-centered and leads us to conclude that we deserve all we can see, touch, or imagine. It creates greedy appetites for far more than we need. We can be released from our self-centered desires by humbling ourselves before God, realizing that all we really need is his approval. When the Holy Spirit fills us, we see that this world's seductive attractions are only cheap substitutes for what God has to offer.

1 Peter 3:9 (NLT)
Don't repay evil for evil. Don't retaliate when people say unkind things about you. Instead, pay them back with a blessing. That is what God wants you to do, and he will bless you for it.

3:8 Peter lists five key elements that should characterize any group of believers: (1) harmony—pursuing the same goals; (2) sympathy—being responsive to others' needs; (3) love—seeing and treating each other as brothers and sisters; (4) compassion—being affectionately sensitive and caring; and (5) humility—being willing to encourage one another and rejoice in each other's successes. These five qualities go a long way toward helping believers serve God effectively.

3:8-9 Peter developed the qualities of compassion and

humility the hard way. In his early days with Christ, these attitudes did not come naturally to his impulsive, strong-willed personality (see Mark 8:31-33; John 13:6-9 for examples of Peter's blustering). But the Holy Spirit changed Peter, molding his strong personality to God's use, and teaching him tenderness and humility.

3:9 In our fallen world, it is often deemed acceptable by some to tear people down verbally or to get back at them if we feel hurt. Peter, remembering Jesus' teaching to turn the other cheek (Matthew 5:39), encourages his readers to pay back wrongs by praying for the offenders. In God's kingdom, revenge is unacceptable behavior, as is insulting a person, no matter how indirectly it is done. Rise above getting back at those who hurt you. Instead of reacting angrily to these people, pray for them.

This study brought revelations that I desperately needed. In the beginning, I believed that God helped those who helped themselves. I believed that God did not answer my prayers. I believed that God did not love me. As I looked back on my prayer life, I realized that he had always been there for me.

Prayer is the most important thing. We should be praying always. God wants a personal relationship with each one of us. What is the single most important thing in any relationship? Communication. God wants to communicate with each of us personally. He wants us to communicate with Him. How do we do that? Talk to Him. Pray!

I had trouble understanding what this meant before my prayer study. I had thought prayer was one-sided. I thought I was supposed to be doing all the talking. I thought I would never know if God was answering. How could I tell if it was Him?

Early in October, shortly after this study, two very significant things happened to change the way I thought about prayer. God gave me a vision during one prayer and answered another one on the day that I asked Him. There is power in prayer, and I am now talking to God all day, every day. I am looking and listening more closely. I am recognizing Him everywhere.

I was praying for my brother and sister one day. They are both in danger of losing their housing. My brother and his wife have five kids and one due in February. My sister and her husband have three kids. I had talked to each of them separately within a week. They both had the same problem and neither knew of the other's problem. They had deadlines to move before the end of this year and had nowhere to go.

I was praying for them constantly. I wasn't worrying anymore because I knew God was going to work out the situation. I was praying that if he was going to use me to help them to let me know how. I don't know why I prayed this, I just felt that he was going to use me somehow. Shortly after praying this, I saw a neighborhood. I saw it so clearly that I started to draw the picture. I had a plan and the idea was to give them each a house as a gift.

I am not sure if you have been paying attention, but without God, I can't help myself. How am I supposed to build these houses and give them as gifts. Well, I guess if that is God's plan, he will show me how. I can tell you that as of right now all I can do is add this to my miracle prayer.

This was a new thing for me, however. I was praying for everyone but me! I was praying for people I saw in public. I was praying for people I saw on TV. I was praying for people I read about in the newspaper. I was praying for everyone else. Some of my prayers had me in tears because I could feel how bad they needed the prayer.

Once again, I ended up back at my vision. I thought if God provides the money for these houses, they should be modest so I can give the money to others as well. The original vision was pretty nice. So, I started talking to God about how to adjust my vision. While I was dreaming with God, the amount of money changed. God had me dreaming with three times the money I needed. What would I do with the money? I told him that I would clear up my problems and the rest needed to be divided up. I needed a certain amount to build the houses. I still had more than a third of the money left.

I could build a small church in the neighborhood. I am still attending church in a senior center. There are four churches that use that facility. There is absolutely nothing wrong with that but I could gift the community with a place of worship. Maybe these churches would rather rent an actual church at a reasonable price. I wonder how many other churches are in the same situation? I know there are two that meet at the high school. Maybe this would be a good idea.

Next, I turned my neighborhood drawing over and started writing ministries' names down. I have to help these ministries more than I am now. They had been very helpful to me during this first year. God really did all of the work but these people are like big brothers and sisters to me. Something I never had and always really wanted. Someone to help show me the way. Now I feel that I have many. Not only that, but I have access to them whenever I want. All I have to do is turn on the television and one of them is there to help me.

My vision was growing, but my doorbell didn't ring with Ed McMahon on the other side. My lottery numbers weren't picked that week. I was not discouraged! I was not worried! God wouldn't have given me that picture if he didn't want me to have everything in the picture. I just thanked God for the vision and figured the answer is not no, the answer is not now. Something to look forward to.

The next week, I had turned on TBN while I was cleaning and I wish I knew what show I was listening to, but Kim Alexis was the guest. She was talking about her kids. She was saying that she was taking them back from the enemy. She talked about having them trapped in the car for a ride somewhere and she planted seeds during the whole ride. Then she said something that made me sit down.

She was talking about praying over their rooms. I had been worried about my youngest daughter all morning and I didn't know why. As I sat and listened, all of a sudden it made perfect sense. In Proverbs 18:21 it says, *"Death and life are in the power of the tongue: and they that love it shall eat the fruit thereof."* There is power when I speak. I can speak God's power over my house.

I immediately started praying out loud. I prayed over the whole house. "The power of life and death is in the tongue," "So, I am saying aloud that the enemy is not allowed to even come into my house," "The enemy can't have my girls," "My girls belong to the Lord," "I have given them to Him," "The enemy can't have Karl and he certainly can't have me," "We belong to the Lord," "The Lord owns this house and he cannot coexist with the enemy," "The enemy can't even enter my home through the smallest crack," "The enemy must stay outside and is not even allowed on my property." "God said, 'I set before you life and death—choose life,' and I chose life for everyone in this home," "This will be a place of refuge."

I walked around the house praying out loud for about a half an hour. I walked into everyone's room and told the enemy he wasn't allowed in these rooms. I started out quietly praying out loud and by the time I was finished I was loud and threatening as I told the enemy to leave my property. I had a moment of doubt and I immediately turned to the Lord and said, "I would appreciate some immediate proof that this prayer was an action prayer. Please show me some sign that what I just prayed was true. Please, I ask this in Jesus' name. Amen."

I'm going to back up a little before I continue. Karl and I had seen a commercial for a movie for the two weeks leading up to this and I never before had this kind of reaction. All I had to do was hear the commercial and my stomach started hurting. I told Karl, "I don't know what is wrong with that movie but I can't see it, there is something about that movie that is really wrong and I can't explain it!"

As I continue, let me tell you that I never noticed that everyone came home in great moods after my praying over the house until later. I went to pick up my youngest daughter at school. I thought, "If I could pray over my home, I could also pray over my car." So, I started the prayer again.

School ended and my daughter got in the car. Everything seemed normal. We talked like normal. There had been no reason to worry about her. Since nothing seemed different, we started home. I was listening to a Christian CD and she asked if she could listen to her music (we usually took turns). I asked her to wait until the song ended and she said okay. I started to turn the volume up and, in my head, I heard, "turn down the music and talk to her." Okay! I turned down the music. I asked her if anything bad had happened that day. She said, "No, everything was fine." I asked her if anything especially good happened that day. She said, "No, everything was fine."

I didn't know what I was looking for and I didn't know what to say. I decided to tell her that I had been praying for her that morning. I told her that I didn't know why but she had been on my mind all day. She said, "Oh, that's cool!" That ended it! I gave up and continued on home.

A couple of minutes later she asked if I would do her a favor. I said, "Maybe." She said she had some homework but she wanted to go to the movies that night. This was her dad's weekend and if she promised to get it done on Saturday, would I not tell her father about the homework. He wouldn't have let her go. I almost said "No" immediately, but something was going on because in my head I kept hearing, "Trust her-Trust her-Trust her!"

I was quiet so long listening in my head that she finally said, "Well?" I said something that I have never said before. I said, "Okay, but I am going to trust you to not let your friends talk you into doing something you know you shouldn't be doing!" Where did that come from? Apparently she was thinking the same thing because she went white!

She asked me if I was psychic. I said, "No. Why?" She looked up at the ceiling of the car. She looked at me to see if I realized what just happened. I am, of course, totally clueless. Then she started to tell me about her day. She said that during first period a friend came to her and asked her if she could go to the movies. The friend said they were all going to buy tickets to one movie and sneak into another movie (the very movie that gave me stomach aches for two weeks!)

My daughter told me that she had said yes to her friend and had a stomach ache and a headache the rest of the day. She told me that she had gone to her desk and secretly prayed that the movie didn't really open that night or that something would go wrong. She had been worried about it all day. She told me that she had planned to tell us that she didn't know what movie she was going to see and they would just buy the tickets when they got there. This way we wouldn't be expecting a review on a movie that she may or may not have seen.

I told her in more detail what I had prayed about that morning, right up to praying that the enemy wasn't even allowed in my car. I told her that she wasn't able to lie because the enemy wasn't there to back her up. She then apologized for planning to lie! I told her that I understood why she did. I normally would have told her no and not listened to an argument. I also wouldn't have explained why I would have told her no. She was 13 and simply had to do what she was told and trust me that it was best for her.

I saw that so clearly and knew that I would not have appreciated that at any age. So I apologized for putting her in a position where she thought she had to lie. I explained that I was trying to become a new person and this was part of the change. I had to look at her like a human being, not just a daughter. She deserved my respect as much as any other human being. Our relationship was forever changed that day. Then we did something we never did before—we prayed.

We prayed that her friends would no longer want to do this,

and even if they did, that God would make my daughter strong enough to lead them away from doing this. Not only that but that they would realize that they actually had more fun doing it her way. We ended the prayer and I asked her how she felt now. She said, "I could do cartwheels right now!"

God even gave me an opportunity to witness to her. I told her that the headache and stomach ache were caused by the Holy Spirit and the enemy having a war. They both wanted her and her choice was going to decide the winner of the war. I told her that she had peace right now because she gave it to God to handle and she was trusting him to do just that.

We got home and I jumped in the shower. I looked back over the day and I could see all the proof that my prayer was answered. I realized that everyone had come home in a good mood. I realized that the enemy had been left at the door. He wasn't allowed to enter into my world that day. He affected my day but he wasn't allowed to succeed in his attempts to destroy my day or anyone else's. I spent the rest of the night thanking God.

Would you like to know what happened with my daughter? I will be happy to tell you! She went to the movie theater and her friends still had every intention of sneaking into this movie. She, however, had already secretly made up her mind not to go along with the crowd. They all decided to buy tickets for a G-rated movie and headed for the ticket taker.

This particular movie theater has two hallways of theaters and therefore has two ticket takers. As they got in line to give their tickets they all realized at the same time that the movie they wanted to sneak into was in the other hallway. They didn't have a ticket for a movie in that hallway. Amazingly, they didn't want to sneak into any other movie and ended up seeing the G-rated movie and had an absolute blast! I was never more proud of my daughter.

God does answer prayers. You just have to trust that the answer will be in the best interest of everyone. I can now look back over a year full of answered prayers. When you pray in line with what he wants for you, he loves to answer prayers. When you finally realize that he wants the best for everyone, you can learn to pray for the right things. When you trust him, you won't be able to count all the ways he has helped you.

Okay, so let's give it a try on something I really need. He didn't give me my vision for no reason. He obviously has a plan to get me my miracle and maybe more. All I have to do is keep my eyes, my mind and my heart open.

THE STALEMATE

*I*have been running what Joyce Meyer said around and around in my mind for months. "If you want your prayers answered, you must be obedient." I started thinking about my life and any areas where I might be slow to act obediently. What am I holding back from God? I have to trust him with everything.

The one thing I kept coming back to was marriage vs. living together. I either had to get married or break up with Karl. This was blatant disobedience in front of a lot of people. Everyone knew we were not married, how could God bless us? I had to get married! God was not holding me back, I was. Karl had mentioned marriage to me in April, and at the time I figured God knew what had been holding us back. He knew our hearts—as soon as we could get married, we would.

I am now in a bit of a quandary! I knew in my heart we were at a stalemate. God had proven over and over that he would answer prayers. He had proven that he loved me and wanted the best for me. He had proven that I was the one that was unfaithful, not Him.

I hadn't wanted to get married until I was sure that I was financially settled, and I could see that I wasn't going to be financially settled until I got married. I can honestly tell you that as I write this, I can feel the fear of the unknown. I have to keep putting the fear away and bringing the trust to the surface.

Karl and I decided we wanted to be obedient more than we wanted our miracle. We wanted our miracle, but we could see the writing on the wall. We would rather trust God. His way works, ours doesn't. We had no idea what he had planned, but we couldn't worry about it anymore.

On October 29th, at one of our dinner dates, we decided to get married as soon as possible. When we got home we called my brother (he was going to be the best man) and my pastor. Our county courthouse performs marriage ceremonies on Wednesdays and this wasn't going to work for anyone. We asked our pastor if he would perform the ceremony at our house on the following Friday, November 5th. He said, "Of course!" and, "it's about time!" We were happy that it was scheduled.

I naturally called my sister (she was going to be the matron of honor). I had forgotten that she was out of town at a women's conference with her church. I ended up talking to my brother-in-law until about 3 a.m. I was in a dead panic! There is no other way to describe it. I was getting ready to do something I had been afraid of doing for five years. I was getting married. I was getting ready to do something I had never really done before. I was going to trust God. Luckily, my brother-in-law talked me down from the ledge and I was very grateful.

By November 1st, I was prepared to buy the marriage license, and we would then have thirty days before it expired. When I got home from the courthouse I realized that I had forgotten about rings. I can't get rings by Friday! I called everyone, and by the end of the day we had changed the date to November 20th. That would give us plenty of time to plan a very casual wedding at our house. We were simply trying to get in line with God's will for our lives and it didn't have to be fancy. After all, in our hearts we had been married for eleven years, we were just going to make it legal.

I was so consumed with worry about this wedding that I was forgetting about the other plans already in place for the month of November. I spent most of my time praying away the worry. God knew this and began to put my mind at ease. He was going to have a battle on his hands.

On November 2nd, I woke up like normal and took my daughter to school and voted. Then I came home and checked my calendar for the day's events. During all the commotion with the impending wedding, I had forgotten that my sister and I had planned to go see Jesse Duplantis in Brandywine, Maryland that night.

The enemy started in on me right away. "You're too tired, it's too far away (2 ½ hour drive), it's too late at night (7 p.m.), you're going to have to go alone, etc." I got up off of the couch after contemplating all of these excuses and started cooking dinner. I had dinner ready for my family by 11:30 a.m. and all they would have to do is heat it up. I was going!!!

Next, I called my sister and asked her if she was still planning to go. She said that with all of the talk about the wedding, she had forgotten to make the necessary arrangements. She still wanted to go with me but she would have to make some phone calls to find baby-sitting. She said she would call me back. She called me back twenty minutes later. Apparently, my dad had walked in just as she was hanging up the phone and agreed to watch the kids as long as she would take notes on the service. She was going!

I picked her up at 4 p.m. We got to the church in plenty of time and had a good seat. We were both in awe. This church was beautiful. Not only that, but it was high-tech. They had camera equipment and sound equipment like I had only seen at concerts. I would expect that in an auditorium setting but not in a church.

The praise and worship was excellent. They had star-quality singers. Then the pastor and his wife came up and prayed. My sister and I couldn't believe what happened next. They asked anyone visiting the church for the first time to stand up because they had some literature for us.

There were probably only about thirty of us standing out of about 200 to 300. While we were still standing, they said a prayer for us and the whole congregation said something in unison. I wish I would have written it down but the gist of it was, "you won't be leaving in the same condition in which you came." I was then being hugged from every direction. I don't get hugged that much at family reunions. The love in that building was so big you could barely carry it around.

Then Jesse Duplantis came up. I won't even try to quote him. There is no way for me to do him justice. I am just not that funny or that blessed, yet. He spent the evening speaking about hopes, dreams and visions. It was no longer a surprise why the enemy had been trying to keep me away. The enemy definitely doesn't want me under the impression that God is on my side.

Jesse started off by asking if we had a vision for our lives. My sister and I looked at each other. He had told us to ask God for a vision. Thinking big was the key. Don't limit God, have faith for bigger things. He spent the night telling us to get God off of the unemployment line. "Give God something to do, tell him your hopes and dreams." I can honestly say that I spent the entire night believing God was speaking directly to me.

My sister and I left with our hope firmly intact. She knows about my vision and is naturally praying for me. We talked all the way home and when I got home I couldn't sleep. I was "faithing" with God. I was "dreaming" with God. I was "believing" with God. The next day, I played the lottery. I still couldn't figure out how God was going to make this happen, but I knew without a doubt that he would.

I was driving to pick up my daughter from school and I was praying for our miracle. I started laughing. I was laughing so hard that I could barely control it. I imagined God saying, "Liz, you are no different than Jesse Duplantis." What a ridiculous thought! He is a very successful minister. He is a blessed man. He is an amazingly blessed man and there is no comparison. Then I imagined God saying, "Liz, I don't love him more than you!" Well, I do know that is true. God is not a respecter of persons. Then I heard it again, "Liz, you are no different than Jesse Duplantis! You could do what he does!"

I was full out belly laughing. I said to myself, "Talk about dreaming!" That sermon last night has gone straight to my head. That must be what is going on in my mind. How could I even think about doing what he does. When it comes to public speaking, I totally sympathize with Moses. God had let Aaron do the speaking for Moses. Who was going to do my speaking?

All of a sudden, however, I could see it as plain as day. God had made other people's hopes, dreams and visions come true, and he could do that for me. I had to remember that God wasn't holding me back, I was holding him back. God doesn't want me to fear him, he wants me to trust him. He will work at my speed. He will go as slow as I want to go or he will go as fast as I want to go. The key is trust. All things are possible, but He won't do anything without trust.

I could see myself doing all kinds of things. I was scared to death but I could see it clearly. I was now praying for him to work at my speed. He had me dreaming of doing things that I wouldn't have thought possible, ever! I was excited but I was still afraid. I wanted to concentrate on my own problems first and dream later. I figured He would show me the way.

That night, I went to Bible study and had the opportunity to talk about what I had heard the night before. I was so excited to talk about it that the whole study was spent debating what I had learned. Some believed and some didn't, but it didn't cause me to waver in any way. I was firm about where I stood in my belief. I even told them that I would be replacing Joyce Meyer when she was ready to retire. Everyone laughed including me! But at least now I knew it was entirely possible.

I came home and again I had trouble sleeping. I was thinking all the time. I couldn't get it to shut off. How was God going to get me my miracle? How was God going to use me? How was God going to get me through this wedding? How was God going to use me? How was God going to get into the hearts of all the people I know? How was God going to use me?

My mind was circling around these questions and I finally prayed that God would help me go to sleep. The not knowing was killing me. I turned on TBN and turned the sound down low and tried to go to sleep. No such luck!

MY MIRACLE

*A*t 12:30 a.m. I had decided I would not be getting any answers and decided to try to go to sleep. TBN was on quietly and I was praying for God to help me go to sleep. They had a praise-a-thon going on and several ministers over several days came on to help raise money. That night, they were having prayers for healing. I didn't really pay much attention to what was going on because I was relatively healthy.

I was just starting to go to sleep when I felt something on my leg. Since I was alone in the room, I was startled. There was no rational explanation for the feeling, it just felt like someone drumming their fingers on my leg. I calmed myself down and again started praying to go to sleep, but now I thought I was losing my mind. While I was laying there praying, a minister had jumped up to the microphone and said, "There is someone out there who needs this. Why are you having trouble believing that God will return to you everything the enemy stole?"

I sat straight up in bed. He went back to his chair. I was devastated! Then they announced that T D Jakes would be preaching shortly. I decided to wait and see if this man would come back with another message for "someone." The healing part of the sermon came to an end and I thought, "what about my message?" Just then, the minister that had jumped to the microphone stood up and was introduced as T D Jakes. I was wide awake and I was thrilled!

He had another person read from the Bible:

2 Kings 6:1-7 (NLT)
One day the group of prophets came to Elisha and told

him, "As you can see, this place where we meet with you is too small. ²Let's go down to the Jordan River, where there are plenty of logs. There we can build a new place for us to meet."

"All right," he told them, "go ahead."

³"Please come with us," someone suggested.

"I will," he said.

⁴When they arrived at the Jordan, they began cutting down trees. ⁵But as one of them was chopping, his ax head fell into the river. "Ah, my lord!" he cried. "It was a borrowed ax!"

⁶"Where did it fall?" the man of God asked. When he showed him the place, Elisha cut a stick and threw it into the water. Then the ax head rose to the surface and floated. ⁷"Grab it," Elisha said to him. And the man reached out and grabbed it.

He explained this story in a way I had never heard. He paralleled the prophets with us and Elisha with God. We were ready for the next step and we wanted God to go with us. We had outgrown where we were and could not go forward without God's permission. God gave his permission and agreed to go with us. We went forward with good intentions but didn't expect to lose our tool. God was going to give us a new tool and bring it within reach. All we would have to do is reach out and grab it.

Now, I am certainly not T D Jakes, but I wrote down most of what was said that night. My notes are as follows:

"God has heard you, he is with you." "He has already started the work on your miracle." "Be patient because it takes a lot of people being obedient to get your miracle to you." "But he is bringing it within reach—just like the axe." "He is taking the seed you sowed (the stick) and supernaturally growing what you need (the axe)." "You're throwing in a stick and you are going to get an axe." "He knows you want to do the work, you just didn't expect to lose the tool." "God is going to give you another axe." "He is already turning it around." "He knows you have a vision without a tool—he'll get you the tool." "Be obedient and be patient." "Elisha went with the servants and God will go with you!"

I was crying so hard by the time he had finished that it took another hour to fall asleep. I know God was talking directly to me. Just like he had the night before. I now know that I don't have to go looking for it, but he is going to bring it to me. How am I going to recognize it? What if I miss it? When is it coming? Help!!!

I woke up the next morning and I started writing down everything I could remember from T D Jakes' sermon the night before. Next, I rewrote the notes from Jesse Duplantis' sermon. The next thing I knew I was writing down everything that had happened to me in the last year. I couldn't write enough. I am not a writer, so these are just notes at this point. I had been writing notes all year long and then putting them on the computer. This was no different.

That night while I was typing up all of my notes, I watched the praise-a-thon again. This time Creflo Dollar was on and his message was similar.

My notes read as follows:

"Don't worry about you." "Seek the kingdom first." "God is not a deadbeat dad." "God provides a way." "Repeat to yourself over and over, 'I am not afraid to prosper, I want to be a distribution center for God, I know what to do with the money.'" "BUILD THE SANCTUARY" "Do the work and God will take care of you." "When lack comes your way say, 'I support the kingdom so I will never be broke another day in my life'."

He was basically saying if you support the kingdom, God

will take care of you, which can be found in Matthew 6:33.

Matthew 6:33 (KJV)
But seek ye first the kingdom of God, and his righteousness; and all these things shall be added unto you.

How do I support the kingdom? I tithe. I contribute financially to several ministries. Then I read the scripture a little more closely. Seek the kingdom of God. Haven't I been doing that for a year now? I've been looking for the kingdom of God all this time. Then God showed me the word "seek" in a different way. He said, "Seek to help the kingdom. Seek to help the whole world know the kingdom!" How do I help anyone else know the kingdom?

I am telling as many people as I can about what I have learned. I am helping everyone I know. How do you help the whole world? No one knows me. I am doing what I know how to do. What more can I do? What do I know how to do? Nothing that would help the world. I continued typing my notes and thinking about what I had heard.

On Sunday, November 7th, Karl and I watched Joel Osteen like we always did. Joel was talking about our thought life. He was explaining that you will only go as far as you can imagine. Are you starting to see a pattern here? He was explaining that your thoughts can hold you back or propel you forward and it's up to you. God won't force anyone. God will come to you where you are.

Karl and I were talking about this and God gave me a vivid picture. I could see God holding the hand of a very small child just learning to walk. A human parent will pull on the child's hand to help the child learn to trust. As the parent pulls on the child's hand, the child will not have a choice but to take a step and hope the parent will not let him fall.

God is not a human parent. God is very patient. He will stand holding your hand for your entire lifetime even if you won't take that step. He will not pull on your hand. He will not force your steps, He will simply guide them. You will have to make the choice to take the step. You will have to be brave and trust Him. Once you have gained your courage, He won't let you fall.

I am going to have to trust Him and take a step.

Okay, God, show me the way!

Now I know what I have to do

I woke up on November 11th and I bought a new notebook and pen and went to breakfast. I had made the decision to take the step. I had been thinking of a way to help others. I don't know what will come of it, but I need to try and I need to trust Him.

I can't be the only Christian who walked away from God. I can't be the only new Christian in the world who is struggling with doubt and disbelief? I can't be the only Christian in the world who doesn't always understand the scriptures and the ministers. I can't be the only Christian in the world who feels like he or she is always behind all the rest of the Christians. I can't be the only Christian who wants to be close to God and doesn't always know how.

Since this is true, I can give others my notes. I can write a book that shows others what I am going through every day. I can let others know that they are not the only ones. I can help others by showing them what God has taught me. I can help others understand that we are all works in progress and none of us will be perfect until we meet Jesus face to face.

I can let others know that I am trusting God, even though I am afraid of doing this. I can let others know that I married Karl on November 20th as planned (without receiving my miracle but trusting God for it). I can let others know that I started this book on November 11th and finished it on November 30th. I can let others know that once I decided to take the step with God, I didn't have one minute of writer's block.

I can let others know that I hated English in school and writing a book was ***never*** on my list of things to do in my life. I can let others know that God will use them in ways they never imagined. I can let others know that I may not know what's in my future, but I am not letting go of God's hand. He will be with me no matter where I go. I will never turn away from him again. I can let others know that he is waiting for them to take the step to be closer to him.

I didn't like my life and now I do. I know there is a purpose for my life even if I don't have the specifics ahead of time. God has shown me things I would never dream about doing and said, "Go ahead!" I have been allowed to make mistakes along the way, and He even taught me from my mistakes.

I am able to look back over my entire life and see Him there always. When I was little, I had my grandmother, aunts and uncles. When I was older and my dad was finally serious about being a Christian, I had him. I rejected him, but I had him. When I was married, he watched over me and didn't let us destroy each other (we are friends to this day). Not only that, but without discussing discipline, we agreed in most areas where our daughters were concerned. The girls still say, "Dad always says that," or, "Mom always says that." When I was on my own, I had Karl. I had found a very best friend. God always put someone there for me.

And finally, when I thought I had lost everything, I finally had God. I invited Jesus back into my life and what a difference a year makes. He has been teaching me lessons all along so that I would be able to look back and realize that he was always there. I realize that I was never in charge. I was never independent. I thank Him for that every day.

He saved me and let me get as far away from Him as I could go. Then he invited me back! Now I get to be a child again! A child of God! I have a heavenly Father that won't let go of my hand while I learn to walk. I want to charge forward with God. What about the rest of the story? Stay tuned.

Thank you, Jesus!!!

Thank you, Heavenly Father!!!

Please don't let go of my hand!!!